About the author

Sarah Ockwell-Smith is the mother of four children. She has a BSc in Psychology and worked for several years in Pharmaceutical Research and Development. Following the birth of her first child, Sarah re-trained as an Antenatal Teacher and Birth and Postnatal Doula. She has also undertaken training in Hypnotherapy and Psychotherapy and is a member of the British Sleep Society. Sarah specialises in gentle parenting methods and is co-founder of the GentleParenting website www.gentleparenting.co.uk. She also blogs at www.sarahockwell-smith.com. Sarah is the author of nine other parenting books: *BabyCalm, ToddlerCalm, The Gentle Sleep Book, The Gentle Parenting Book, Why Your Baby's Sleep Matters, The Gentle Discipline Book, The Gentle Potty Training Book, The Gentle Eating Book* and *The Second Baby Book*. She frequently writes for magazines and newspapers, and is often called upon as a parenting expert for national television and radio.

THE STARTING SCHOOL BOOK

SARAH OCKWELL-SMITH

How to choose, prepare for and
settle your child at school

piatkus

PIATKUS

First published in Great Britain in 2020 by Piatkus

1 3 5 7 9 10 8 6 4 2

A CIP catalogue record for this book
is available from the British Library.

ISBN 978-0-349-42379-1

Typeset in Stone Serif by M Rules
Printed and bound in Great Britain by
Clays Ltd, Elcograf S.p.A

Papers used by Piatkus are from well-managed forests
and other responsible sources.

Piatkus
An imprint of
Little, Brown Book Group
Carmelite House
50 Victoria Embankment
London EC4Y 0DZ

An Hachette UK Company
www.hachette.co.uk

www.improvementzone.co.uk

Note The information provided on childhood illnesses is not
intended to replace any advice given to you by your GP or other
health professional. If you have any concerns about your child's
health, contact the appropriate health professional. The author
and publisher disclaim any liability directly or indirectly from
the use of the material in this book by any person.

Sic Itur Ad Astra

Contents

Introduction

The average child spends around 21,000 hours of their life at school. This accounts for just under 15 per cent of most people's childhood. It goes without saying, then, that choosing the best school for your child is a big deal. In fact, it may just be the most important choice you will ever make regarding their present and future happiness. Given the weight of this decision, many parents feel confused about their options and what to look for when choosing a school. The most important points can get lost in a sea of professionally printed prospectuses, slick websites, open days, government statistics, league tables and comparison sites.

The challenge of choosing a school for their child brings many questions for parents: what should they ask when going to visit? What are their legal rights regarding starting age and either sending or not sending their child to school? How important is class size? What about state versus public school? Single or mixed sex? And are there any alternative schooling options? So many questions, but so few resources to help them wade through all the possibilities. How ironic that there are whole magazines, websites and even television shows dedicated to choosing a car or buying a house, yet little to no advice when it comes to selecting schools for our children – a decision that is just as important, if not more so, than the material ones we must make in our lives.

Knowing what to look for in a school and ensuring a good fit with your child's needs is essential, and understanding the official reports and statistics and asking the right questions (of the right people) are key. That is why Chapter 3 cuts right through the noise and confusion to provide clarity in helping you to make the very best choice for your unique and individual child. Because what is right for one child won't necessarily be right for another.

Deciding on a school is only part of the picture though. What happens once you have made your choice? Again, confusion reigns as to when and how to apply and how to navigate the system – from admission criteria and applications to deadlines and acceptance. All this and everything in between is covered in Chapter 2.

Once you know which school your child will be attending and when, thoughts move on to getting them ready. How you prepare your child for school in the months before they start and help them to settle in can have a huge impact on their early months and years. A child who is happy when starting school is usually one who is happy to learn – and a happy learner in the early years is one of the most important predictors for academic success later in life. So what sort of emotional preparation will help children to feel confident and happy when they start school, so that they may handle the change with relative ease? And what sort of emotional preparation do you, the parent, need, so that you transition well too? In Chapter 4 you will find all the information you need on supporting your child in making new friends, forming a good relationship yourself with both the school and other parents, dealing with separation anxiety (theirs and your own) and other settling-in issues, so that the move to school is as calm and as easy as possible for your child and the whole family.

Practical preparation can be as crucial as the emotional kind and Chapter 4 will deal with that too, covering everything under the banner of 'school readiness' – what you need to teach your child (and, perhaps more importantly, what you don't) in order to place them on an equal footing with their peers and give them a flying start. Uniform and equipment will also be discussed – what you really need and what you don't; and why, often, more expensive doesn't equal better. From there, Chapter 5 will take you to the next stage – the first day and settling in: everything you should know about making your child's early school experience as positive and as enjoyable as it can be.

Of course, no book about school would be complete without a section on how children learn – because if we don't understand that, well, how can we possibly make good choices around their education? Chapter 1 focuses on exactly that – the many factors that can influence a child's learning: when they are ready for school, physically and psychologically, whether they learn best with others of their own age, with same-sex peers or mixed classes, whether the size of a school or class affects them and what they need to help them thrive. It also looks at how special educational needs and disabilities (SEND) affect learning and any special consideration that children with SEND may need. All of these need to be thought through before making that all-important choice.

Sometimes our best-laid plans don't pan out as we hope, and for this reason Chapter 6 focuses on common concerns that parents have: what to do if your child finds it hard to settle in, has difficulty separating from you, friendship issues or plain refusal to go to school; how to help them if you feel that they are not being stretched enough or, conversely, they are struggling with the workload; some of the medical issues that frequently crop up at school, and what to do about them – for instance, the dreaded head lice and contagious diseases that seem to spread like wildfire among children.

In Chapter 7, we'll look at the social side of children attending school, with a special focus on how parents can get involved with the school community – because the best education happens when both children and parents are well engaged with the school. Chapter 8 takes things into the future a little, looking ahead to the next few years at school and how you can raise your child to be an inspired learner, especially when homework and standardised tests start to rear their heads.

As well as including the most current and relevant research findings in the book, along with my own experiences of school as a mother of four school-aged children, I have also asked for advice from those who matter the most: parents who have been there and teachers who live the transition every year. There are tips and advice from fellow parents and early-years teachers throughout the book, but Chapter 9 focuses on the things that parents wish they'd known before their children started school, as well as what teachers wish parents of new starters knew. Valuable advice indeed.

Some of us (myself included) view our school days as among the best of our lives. I absolutely loved my time at school, particularly the early years. For others, however, their time at school is not looked back on so fondly. My ultimate goal when writing this book, was to enable parents to help their children fall into the former category, providing a positive, calm and happy school experience. The school years aren't just about children though; this is a big transition for parents too, and so my goal is also to leave you feeling reassured and excited about what lies ahead and all that it brings. Because the best school years happen when both children and their parents feel happy and engaged with the whole experience.

A quick note on using this book

Each chapter of this book is designed to be free-standing. If you are reading at the early stages of thinking about your child's education or applying for a school place, I recommend starting with Chapters 1 through 3 and returning to the later chapters around the time you receive notification of your child's school place. If you are at the stage of preparing your child for starting school, having already received notification of a school place, I'd advise you to read Chapters 4 through to 7, as well as Chapter 9. Finally, if your child has actually started school and you would like some help with smoothing the transition, I'd suggest reading Chapters 7 through 9. There is, however, information throughout the book that you should find helpful at any point.

For those reading outside the United Kingdom, the information in Chapter 2 covers application procedures and policies for the UK only, but all other chapters are relevant regardless of where in the world you live.

Chapter 1

Factors that Influence Children's Learning – and How to Be Mindful of Them

Childhood, at its very essence, is all about learning, with play as the primary vehicle for teaching. Children do not need formal education to take an interest in and make sense of the world – they are innately driven to explore, experiment and practise. The biggest driver of learning is not something we do to them, or even necessarily with them, but their natural curiosity. That said, you have been teaching your child since the day they were born. You have been, and always will be, their greatest teacher. This teaching happens entirely naturally, often when you don't even realise it is occurring. The same is true of a child's natural learning – you do not need to do anything or send children anywhere to make this happen.

School is not necessary for children to learn, but modern-day life and society have positioned it in such a way that most parents now don't feel qualified to teach their children. School should be an extension of a child's innate and natural learning drive, not a replacement for it. The best schools will work with a child's natural curiosity and interests, to further them and build on the wonderful pool of knowledge they have already acquired.

This chapter will consider how your choice of school can impact on your child's learning, both now and in the future. While children are innately primed to learn, there are certain elements at school that can affect this drive, both positively and negatively. For instance, class size and the abilities and ages of the other children. Parents may worry that their efforts at home will be in vain if school teaches in a different way; therefore, home life versus school life will also be discussed. The effect of school starting age is another key factor when deciding if your child is ready or not. All of these need to be taken into account in making a mindful and informed decision about your child's education.

Learning in early childhood is heuristic, meaning that children learn by doing and experiencing things for themselves. Early learning should be hands-on, messy, fun and active, incorporating nature and the outdoors as much as possible. Too often when we think of school, we think of children sitting in rows at desks, staring at blackboards or completing worksheets in silence. Thankfully, this is not what happens in the early years of school, although it is, sadly, a fitting description of school life as children approach adolescence. The early years of school revolve around play and movement, experimentation, fun and creativity, rather than formal teaching. Although there is a focus on communication, language, literacy, mathematics, physical and social development in the school curriculum, these can all be learned in a relaxed, child-friendly and child-led way, amid play, noise, fun and movement.

The different stages of learning

Childhood is usually divided into four distinct phases of learning, based upon the work of the Swiss psychologist Jean Piaget's Theory of Cognitive Development:

1. **Sensorimotor stage: birth to two years** In this highly sensory stage, babies predominantly learn about the world and themselves via their senses and interactions with their caregivers and environment. These help them to form what are known as 'schemas' – sets of stored knowledge and information about related objects and experiences. As the babies grow, new experiences are assimilated into existing schemas, or new schemas are formed or adapted to accommodate them. These schemas become the building blocks of knowledge about the world in which the babies live.

2. **Preoperational stage: two to seven years** At this stage, children are very self-centred (referred to as 'egocentric') and lacking in rational (or what is formally known as 'concrete') thinking. They very much focus on learning tangible facts, through things that they can touch and see – for example, learning basic maths (such as addition and subtraction) and classifying the world through simple facts. During the preoperational stage, school focuses on growing happiness and confidence in learning, in preparation for more formal learning in the future. Teachers will be focusing on developing skills

such as social and emotional intelligence, language and communication, literacy, independence, fine motor skills and fostering curiosity, encouraging children to ask questions about the world around them.

3. **Concrete operational stage: seven to twelve years** During this stage, egocentrism lessens, as the child begins to develop more empathy and understanding of the different ways that others think and feel. Rational and hypothetical thinking and reasoning skills increase, meaning children can learn about the world and the way it works in a more abstract and philosophical sense. Logical thought processes develop during this stage, thus supporting the ability to interact with a more formal, or academic, style of teaching.

4. **Formal operational stage: eleven years through adolescence** This stage of development is all about theoretical, philosophical and hypothetical thinking and the child's ability to ask big questions about the world and others in it. This is the time to learn about the whys, the hows and the what-ifs of life. Learning in adolescence becomes more strategic, as older children and teenagers can grasp the most abstract of concepts.

What do children need to learn well?

In 1943, the American psychologist Abraham Maslow published his Theory of Human Motivation. This contained what is now famously known as Maslow's Hierarchy of Needs. The Hierarchy of Needs details five distinct stages that individuals need to go through in order to reach their full potential – something Maslow termed 'self-actualisation'. The Hierarchy of Needs is commonly depicted as a triangle, the pinnacle of which is self-actualisation and the base starts with the most rudimentary, yet most important, needs that must be fulfilled in order to build on the foundations to move up to the next level.

Before we can focus on learning, we first need to make sure that children are safe, have all of their physical needs met and feel a sense of security and belonging in the world; in other words, that they feel loved and nurtured at home and have a good relationship with the adults taking care of them at school. Once these base layers are taken care of, children can move up to forming good peer relationships, making friends and taking pride in their own learning and achievements. When all these stages are fulfilled, children can reach their potential as learners. If the needs at any one stage are not fully met, then this cannot happen.

What does Maslow's Hierarchy tell us about what children need to learn? Ultimately, they need to feel safe, supported, nurtured, connected and accepted by their caregivers and peers, both at home and at school. These needs are far more important than any individual aspects of the school curriculum or the school itself. If they are met, then the child is almost certain to do well; if they are not, then no number of clever teaching techniques, impressive equipment, new buildings, imaginative curriculums, high official ratings and scores or small class sizes will help. The needs of a young learner are really simple when you strip them back to basics.

Growth mindset theory

Psychologist Carol Dweck, a professor at Stanford University in the USA, is famed for her powerful model for enhancing motivation, as featured in her 2006 book, *Mindset*. Dweck's theory states that success and achievement are based not on innate or genetic ability, but upon the individual's *beliefs* surrounding their ability to achieve. The two mindsets are known as 'fixed' and 'growth'. The table below summarises the main differences.

Fixed Mindset	Growth Mindset
Believes abilities are innate, or genetic, and that there is little to nothing that can be done to change them.	Believes that abilities can always be improved – that they are not fixed – with hard work and determination.
Failure is an indication of not being good enough, thus it is taken badly and children are often scared of it.	Failure is an indication of not having tried hard enough and thus is not taken badly. Instead, it is welcomed as a learning opportunity.

Gives up easily when thinking a task is too hard.	Determined and focused on a task that is challenging, sticking with it until it is mastered.
Says things like: 'I can't do this. I'm not good enough. I should just give up.'	Says things like: 'I can't do this *yet*. I believe I can if I really try and work hard though.'

The theory of mindset applies equally to both adults and children, although it is especially pertinent when you consider schooling. Mindsets are by no means permanent; it is possible to change from one to another, and individuals commonly alternate between the two over time. Children will not usually be conscious of the mindset they hold most often, although educating them about the idea can help them to become more so. Unsurprisingly, research has found that children who predominantly exhibit a growth mindset are more likely to work hard, especially in the face of obstacles, which can lead to greater academic success and fulfilment.[1]

The way in which adults speak to and act around children can also impact their mindset. Praising a child may seem a good way to increase self-esteem; however, research has shown that it is more likely to produce a fixed mindset and incentivise children with extrinsic (external) motivation, meaning that the child's intrinsic (or internal) drive for mastery and success is damaged. In order to encourage a growth mindset, children need to feel good about their ability to work hard and achieve success.[2] This feeling of pride in their capacity to stick with a task that they may have found hard initially drives intrinsic motivation, increasing the likelihood that they will work hard and stick at a task in the future.

How to encourage a growth mindset

The following tips can help to foster a growth mindset in children, particularly when they start school:

- When a child succeeds at something, encourage them to think about what helped them to complete the task successfully and how they should use this knowledge next time.

- Empathise with your child's frustration, but don't try to fix things for them in order to prevent it.

- Show your child that you have noticed and appreciate their determination to complete a task.

- Celebrate mistakes and point out your own to help normalise them and allow your child to see them as a sign of learning.

- Keep your expectations of your child age-appropriate, while encouraging them to aim for aspirational goals.

- Don't praise achievements; rather, praise the process and the hard work the child put in.

- Try not to use generic praise, such as 'good boy' or 'well done'; instead, focus on a specific praise that describes what your child is doing and helps them to feel seen and appreciated for their efforts. For example, 'You really have worked hard at that picture; I've been watching you draw the trees so carefully'.

- Model a growth mindset yourself: talk to your child about your efforts and perseverance and how they have helped you to achieve your goals.

- Be mindful of your own language: don't say things like 'I can't do it, I'm useless!' Instead, say, 'I'm struggling right now, but I think I can do it if I work at it'.

SCHOOL OR PARENTS – WHICH HAS THE MOST IMPACT AND INFLUENCE ON CHILDREN?

While a child's experience at school invariably shapes them, the primary influence in their life and on their development is time spent with their parents. In the Introduction, I mentioned that children spend approximately 21,000 hours of their lives at school. When you think that childhood (birth to eighteen years) is around 157,000 hours, approximately 65,000 of which are spent asleep, that still leaves a huge 71,000 waking hours spent with parents, family members and other close caregivers. In other words, children spend three quarters of their childhood (waking hours) outside of school. So what you do, as parents, before your child starts school, and in the hours outside of school once they have started, will always matter the most when it comes to shaping the character and personality of your child.

I am often asked what parents should do if the way they raise their children is at odds with the way schools do things, and even whether school is a good idea at all if they are following a more natural or gentle approach to parenting. My standard response is to remember that you are always the primary influence in your child's life, and children are resilient and flexible enough to cope with the differences between home and school. The same is true of childcare too. Of course, this does not mean that it doesn't matter which education choice you make, or how you help your child to settle and tackle any problems that may arise; it just means that you have more impact than you may have realised.

Do boys and girls learn differently?

There is a pervasive myth in our society that girls are quieter and more studious and, as a result, cleverer than boys. Also, that boys are more likely to have issues at school because they find it harder to sit still, be quiet and concentrate. And it is also believed that boys are less mature than girls and that this immaturity negatively affects their learning, especially in the early years. These are all erroneous beliefs that, sadly, tend to spawn a self-fulfilling prophecy. By preschool age, girls are indeed showing superior social skills to boys; however, when we look at the way in which girls and boys are parented, there are clear differences: girls are spoken to more than boys and emotions are encouraged, while boys are supported in being more active and presumed to be better programmed for physical achievements. Even teachers show bias based on gender, with research showing that they are more likely to reward girls than boys, regardless of actual abilities. A girl is also more likely to receive higher grades for her work, even if it is at the same level as that of a boy.[3]

It is true that there are clear differences in achievement between girls and boys at the end of their schooling, with girls tending to attain higher grades and more qualifications, as well as demonstrating superior behaviour to boys. Boys are more likely to take up STEM subjects (science, technology, engineering and maths) than girls and they are also more likely to achieve either very highly, or very poorly, in these subjects. Underachieving and low grades are much more common in boys across all subjects, as are behaviour issues, with boys accounting for over 80 per cent of all school exclusions.[4] This is not due to biological differences though. Almost all differences in educational achievement, based upon the child's sex, occur as a result of our biases and the overly gender-stereotyped views and actions of society. Trying to avoid perpetuating these biases ourselves, especially when our children are young, is so important if we wish to break this cycle in education. Of course, the first step is to recognise that they do exist. Our own upbringings and the views of our parents (passed on by their parents, in turn) produce a subconscious inherited lineage of labelling. What we say, do and believe regarding gender difference is so often the result of how we were treated ourselves. But by being mindful of these patterns through our own thoughts and actions we can begin to break these stereotypes. (See page 219 for useful resources.)

Single- or mixed-sex schools?

The jury is still out on whether or not single-sex schooling is beneficial for children. There is a lack of evidence showing consistent harm or benefit and there does not appear to be a consensus view based upon the current body of research. The main benefit of single-sex schooling is that there is far less chance that subject choices and achievement will be influenced by gender stereotyping. For instance, girls are more likely to take (and do well in) STEM subjects in a girls-only school than they are in a co-educational (mixed-sex) setting. The biggest downside of single-sex schools seems to be that they create an artificial social environment and may hinder social skills with the opposite sex. There is also a widespread belief that boys flourish in mixed-sex schools, thanks to the calming presence of girls, whereas girls do better at single-sex schools, due to the lack of disruption from boys. While there is limited evidence to support this,[5] there is equally evidence showing that this belief is once again based on outdated gender stereotypes and is simply not true.[6] Any other apparent benefits or downsides could also be down to current social stereotyping and not attributable to school demographics at all.

Male or female teachers – does it matter?

Early-years schooling has become increasingly feminised. Currently, in the UK, two thirds of all teachers are female. However, in early-years teaching, over 80 per cent of all teachers are female.[7] This disparity leaves a real gap in the early-school environment, with numerous children not encountering a male teacher until they enter high school. Many parents believe that this lack of a male role model at school is problematic for young boys, but this is not an evidence-based claim, researchers having found no difference in outcomes for children taught by teachers of the same sex as them, versus the opposite.[8] Further research, specifically concerned with the relationships between students and teachers, found that while female teachers reported better relationships with their students, both male and female teachers reported more difficult relationships with boys than with girls,[9] indicating that male teachers are not necessarily better for boys in terms of building a strong relationship or providing a male role model. This, of course, does not mean that the lack of male teachers in schools should not be addressed. A mix of both adult males and females provides children with a more accurate representation of society and a more holistic schooling experience. However, when it comes to relationships and what is best for children, it's likely to come down to individual teachers and their unique attributes, rather than gender.

Does class size matter?

Class size is a hot topic when choosing a school. Most parents seem to prefer smaller class sizes, the perceived wisdom being that the smaller the class, the more individual attention a child will receive – this often being considered more conducive to learning and better outcomes. Smaller class sizes are also often cited as one of the benefits of private over state schooling. Does it really matter though?

Confusingly, the evidence is not as clear cut as you might think. Smaller classes do seem to have a modest impact on learning, their pupils being a few months ahead; however, this difference (in terms of both academic achievement and behaviour) is only significant when the class size is *very* small – i.e. eighteen pupils or fewer. There is far less difference in outcome when you look at a class size of between twenty and thirty-five children, the theory being that when class sizes are very small teachers adapt their teaching style to suit the small group, but when the class size is bigger the approach to teaching is very similar, whether there are twenty or thirty-five children. So teaching style seems to matter just as much as class size.[10]

Another issue that is not taken into account as much as I think it should be is how small class sizes can prove problematic for making friends. If your child is one of, say, fifteen children in a class, they have a much smaller pool of children to bond with, so there is less scope for them to form a close friendship with a like-minded individual than if they are in a class of thirty. A larger class size, therefore, can often make forming friendships easier for children.

What about mixed-age classes?

Some schools, particularly smaller ones, merge two or more different year groups into one class. This mostly occurs because of simple economics – where classes are very small it is not viable to run them individually. Sometimes schools choose to run mixed-age classes in the belief that they are more beneficial to children, the theory being that children all have a unique ability that is not defined by their age. Avoiding single-age classes can allow a child to be taught to their true ability, rather than what's deemed appropriate based on their age.

Common concerns from parents about mixed-age classes include worries that the younger children will find the work too difficult and thus won't be engaged and any problems will be overlooked. Parents of older children worry that their children won't be stretched enough, if they are working at the level of the younger children in the class. The fact is, however, that children should all be taught at their level of knowledge and ability – not too easy, but not too difficult – and mixed-age classes do not hinder this in any way.

Perhaps the main positive of these classes is better social-ising with children of different ages, bringing out nurturing behaviour in the older children and boosting confidence in the younger ones. Research has consistently found that children are not academically disadvantaged by them, but they can improve social skills.[11] Other benefits of mixed-age classes are that they can help older children who may be struggling to not feel that they are at the bottom of the class and stretch the younger children who are more able. Mixed-age classes can also provide more opportunity for forging friendships. The biggest downside with a mixed-age class is size, when combining years to make one large class.

Special educational needs and disabilities

Special educational needs and disabilities (SEND for short) is a term used to apply to children who have additional needs which impact on their learning experience. Some SEND children will have learning difficulties or social skills which can impact their learning, such as attention deficit hyperactivity disorder (ADHD) and dyslexia. Others may have a physical disability which does not directly impact their learning capabilities but may make life trickier at school. Research has shown that as many as four in ten children will be identified as having a SEND between starting school at age four or five and age eleven.[12]

SEND children often need additional support at school to aid their learning. The support varies based upon the specific needs of the child, from a one-to-one helper to the provision of accessible learning materials, behavioural interventions, social and emotional learning support and special considerations for the day-to-day school routine (an extra or longer break time, for example). Each school should have a dedicated special educational needs coordinator (SENCo), whose role it is to ensure that children with SEND have the appropriate help at school, through special plans and discussions with parents and other school staff and external professionals. The SENCo is also likely to be involved if a previously undiagnosed child is suspected of having a SEND once they start school.

If your child has already been diagnosed with, or you suspect they have a SEND, then school choice needs to be considered carefully, as, sadly, not all schools are equal when it comes to SEND support. This is something that will be discussed further in Chapter 3.

When are children ready for school?

The age at which children are ready for formal learning is another hotly disputed topic. Around the world, school starting ages range from as low as three years old (in France and Hungary, for example) to seven (in Denmark, Estonia, Finland, Poland and Sweden).

So what are the pros and cons of an early school starting age? The table below summarises the main points:

Pros	Cons
A reduction in childcare bills for working parents.	Children may not be ready to leave their parents, or primary caregiver, and may find the separation difficult.
Some children are ready for school at an early age and thrive in a more formal environment with their peers.	Poorer and more disruptive behaviour in the classroom, due to the relative immaturity of the children.
May slightly raise IQ levels.	No significant improvement in academic outcomes, despite the extra years at school.

Let's look at some of these issues in a little more detail.

Starting age and behaviour and focus

Research from Stanford university has found that delaying the start of school from six to seven years in Danish children has a dramatic impact on reducing inattention.[13] This is not only apparent when the children start school, but also appears to last for several years, still being noticeable at age eleven. It makes sense that starting school at a later age improves attention because as the brain develops and matures with age, so does the child's behaviour.

Starting age and academic achievement

There is research to show that school starting age does appear to impact on academic achievement, with children who start at a later age tending to outperform those who start younger in tests.[14] The counterargument is that because the children are being tested when they are older they therefore have an increased cognitive ability. But, confusingly, there are also studies which show a slight reduction in IQ levels (as opposed to school-based tests) for children who start school later.[15]

Starting age and mental health

There is some evidence that starting school later is beneficial to a child's mental health.[16] One study linked mental-health difficulties in middle age with an early school starting age,[17] while another found that children from low socio-economic backgrounds developed more social and emotional problems if they started formal school early, compared to remaining in a free-play nursery setting.[18] These effects lasted well beyond childhood, with those who had attended formal school early being less likely to hold down a job and more likely to commit crime than their peers who spent longer in a more relaxed learning environment.

Starting age and learning to read and write

One area in which parents are concerned about a later school starting age, is the teaching of reading and writing. Here, the science is clear that there is no reason for concern. Research comparing the outcomes of children who learn to read and write at either five or seven years of age found that while the literacy skills of those who began formal tuition earlier is initially superior, any difference has entirely disappeared by the age of eleven.[19] Or, in other words, those who start learning to read and write later catch up quickly.

How to reach a decision about the best starting age for your child

To answer this, we need to look at both the research (which tends to indicate that later is better) and the individual child and their needs – because research only paints one half of the picture, and while data can tell you about the outcome for other children, the scientists have never met *your* child, so you must always consider what you know about your own child and what you feel is best for them.

Sometimes parents instinctively know that the later their child starts school, the better it will be for them or, conversely, they can sense school readiness at a young age. My own children were all very different. My firstborn, a summer-born boy, was absolutely not ready to start school two months after his fourth birthday. We tried, but it became obvious almost instantly that he needed more time to mature, both physically and emotionally. I negotiated with the school to send him part-time, from 9 a.m. to 12.30 p.m., until the last term of the school year, when he turned five. Only then did he attend full-time. On the other hand, my second-born, an autumn baby, was desperate to go to school and it became apparent that he was more than ready a good six months before he actually started. The six-month wait was filled with frustration for all of us and we felt such relief when he finally started. He took to school like a duck to water, having waited for what felt like an eternity for his start date. My third-born, a winter baby, had a lukewarm start to school, not bad, but not great either; and my fourth, an April baby, was the most school ready of them all, despite having only just turned four a few months before starting.

In my work with parents, I sometimes come across a mis-match between children's and parental needs and views. Some parents can carry a lot of anxiety about their child starting school and perceive them as not being ready when, in fact, the child is more than ready and will thrive. In this case, the paren-tal anxiety can hold the child back. Others, in their eagerness to reclaim some 'me-time' or to reduce childcare costs (under-standably), are slightly blind to the fact that their child would probably do better staying home for longer.

The simple fact is: you can read all the research in the world, but ultimately your child is unique. Be guided by the facts and figures, but don't let them overshadow what is best for your child. If the evidence and your instinct agree, then hopefully it will make you more secure in your choice, but don't be concerned if what you feel is right is at odds with the evidence, or with what others do. You know your child better than anybody else, so don't let them dent your confidence in what you believe to be true.

Compulsory school starting age and delaying entry

Regardless of when children may be eligible to start school, they do not need to be in full-time education until they are of compulsory school age (CSA). In the UK, CSA ranges between four and five and a half years old, depending on which country you live in (see the next chapter for the specifics). In England and Wales, for example, the child is not of CSA until the beginning of the term after they turn five years of age; however, many children in England and Wales will start school when they have only just turned four – a whole year earlier than they legally need to be there. CSA obviously varies in other countries around the world, from as low as three to as high as seven years of age.

Is it beneficial to delay the school start for summer-born children?

Many parents struggle with children, particularly summer-born ones (those born between 1 April and 31 August) starting school before they are ready, not realising that there is no legal obligation for their child to actually be in full-time education until they reach CSA.

A lot of newly turned four-year-olds have barely grown out of nappies, with some still napping during the day, and so starting school, particularly full-time, at such a young age can be troublesome and difficult. Delaying their start to compulsory school age is, therefore, an easily reached decision for many parents. Research gathering data from 2000 primary schools in England and Wales over a five-year period shows that being the youngest in the school year can put children at a significant disadvantage from an educational attainment point of view, particularly with reading and mathematics test scores.[20] While the attainment gap between summer-born children and their older peers does decrease as they all get older, there is still a distinguishable gap in achievement by the last year of primary school.

Given the potential disadvantage posed by being summer-born, you would think that the idea of delaying entry until after a child's fifth birthday would be embraced by all who work in education. But the evidence for and against summer-born starting delays is annoyingly contradictory. A recent government study found that delaying school entry for summer-born children in England has little impact on their academic achievement.[21] The researchers focused on children's scores from tests in phonics (a method used to teach reading and writing) performed in Year 1 (the second year of school in England) and found that summer-born children whose start had been deferred a year only did marginally better than their counterparts who started school when they had just turned four. The difference was so small that it was not considered to be statistically significant. This research has been heavily criticised though, for excluding the test scores of children with special educational needs (arguably those who might benefit the most from a delay) and also because the focus was solely on academic test scores, taking no account of the impact of delaying entry on mental health, wellbeing, behaviour, social interactions and intrinsic motivation to learn. Leaving these out of the research seems naïve and short-sighted, throwing the validity of the research findings into question. Parents of summer-born children rarely cite academic achievement as a concern when choosing to delay entry. Their reasons are usually related to the social and emotional wellbeing of their children, as these parents say:

We delayed our August-born son's start because we came to realise that there is no substitute for time! In particular, time to play and learn without the restrictions the school system brings.

We wanted to delay our August-born daughter's start date because school is not what it used to be. With all the testing, we feel it's a tougher journey now than it was for us. We thought she would be more able to face that journey when she was a year older.

I delayed the start for my May-born son. There were several reasons for it. My conviction is that four is way too early to start formal school. The other reasons for delay were to do with my son himself. We felt he was emotionally immature and wouldn't be able to keep his head above water. It took him several months to settle into preschool, and for a long time he cried and clung on to me at drop-off. We were also having trouble with potty training and, in general, held the belief that he would benefit from an additional year of unstructured play and learning.

I delayed the school start for my August-born son (but born two months prematurely, he was not due to arrive until October) because I wanted him to be given the opportunity to excel and thrive at school, rather than just get by. I think it's by far the best decision I have made as a parent.

I didn't delay school entry for my daughter, born in June, because she was showing me she was ready for school. She loved nursery and was doing well there. I feel for her; it was the right choice.

I didn't delay school for my daughter (born at the end of August). She was excited about going, and the school had a mixed Reception/Year 1 class, which meant she was in the same class as her older sister. Also, the school would have enabled her to go part-time if needed (she didn't need it) and they ensure that children learn at their own level, so she wasn't being measured up to other kids much older.

We didn't delay our end-of-July-born daughter's school start because she was very much ready for big school. She had been in full-time nursery since she was nine months old and has run with older children and learned so much from them. She didn't struggle with the move at all.

We didn't delay our late-July-born son's start, mostly due to social reasons. He had a lovely group of friends at preschool and it felt right for us that they all moved up to Reception together. My son is a very social creature and I think he would have really found it hard being the only one not to move up.

If you feel that you would like to consider delaying school entry for your own summer-born child, the next chapter discusses the practicalities of how to do this, and the Resources section (see page 219) lists sources that can provide support and information.

Alternatives to mainstream education

Although there is a compulsory starting age (CSA) for a child to receive a full-time education, in many countries this does not have to be within a formal school setting and it can occur at home – known as home-schooling, or home-education. Home-education is legal in the UK and Ireland, as well as in Australia, Canada, New Zealand, South Africa and the USA and many other countries. Unfortunately, it is illegal in some countries, including Germany, Greece, the Netherlands, Sweden, Turkey and Brazil.

While this book is about starting school, I felt it would be a good idea to include a small section on home-education for those who are not entirely sold on the idea of school but may not have realised that there is an alternative. It is estimated that 60,000–80,000 children are home-educated in the UK at the time of writing, a figure that has almost doubled over the last half a decade. Home-education is very much on an upward trajectory and is a valid alternative to mainstream schooling. Parents choose to home-educate their children for many different reasons:

Both my husband and I struggled in school. He was expelled before his exams, and my school hated that I was chatty and asked lots of questions. I couldn't bear my son being told off for having a question. My boy is very spirited and loves the outdoors, so Forest School and home-schooling are for us. Mainstream school is no place for his personality.

We home-educate mainly because I see no reason not to! Our family life can fortunately accommodate it. It means, as the facilitators, we can follow our child's interests and expand on them. I also have a problem with early-years testing and discipline methods used commonly in schools. Happily, we can avoid these aspects at home too.

Our decision to home-educate was mostly based on what we feel is the incompatibility of the current school system with how children learn best. Home-education can be tailored to what works for the individual child. I've worked with children my entire working life and I've seen the negative effects that a 'one-size-fits-all' system can have on some of them.'

I don't think our education model is based on what is best for children. I believe that home-education is infinitely more flexible, enjoyable and meaningful than the limited time, space or one-to-one input that a school can provide. I used to teach and almost the entire day was based around crowd control, shuffling kids back and forth to different rooms or seating arrangements and handing out or collecting in. Actual time spent imparting any decent amount of knowledge was very thin on the ground.

I have taught my son how to walk, talk and do many of life's other vital things; I feel no one else is more qualified or invested in the education and happiness of my child, than I am. So, we will go on this journey together learning in a natural way.

We realised early on that we'd be able to provide a totally tailor-made education based on our child's development and interests at home, and it made much more sense to us to do that than to have our child be one of thirty, all learning exactly the same thing at the same time. It's a bonus to be able to avoid bullying, the stress of tests and school discipline systems.

Home-education was clearly the right choice for these families, and it may be for you too. However, I do feel it is possible to give children an enjoyable, happy and successful education in school too. Both options have their own hurdles and difficulties that need to be managed with care, but both very much have a place in the style of parenting that I promote – gentle, authoritative parenting (characterised by parental warmth and nurturing).

If home-education is something that you would like to consider, your starting point, ideally, should be to talk to other parents who home-educate in your area or near by. They will be able to fill you in on local support, activities and meet-up groups, as well as pointers for local learning opportunities – for instance, many museums and historical properties run special events for those who home-educate. A strong local home-education network can provide your child with many opportunities to socialise with other children of all ages (including their own), meaning they miss out on none of the socialisation of school (a common myth and fear surrounding home-education, which is almost always unfounded). See page 219 for some resources and reading recommendations if you would like to find out more about the ethos and theories of home-education and the practicalities of starting it.

Hopefully, this chapter has helped you to understand that education, ultimately, is personal for each family. While the experiences of others, research and statistics can help to guide your decisions, nobody knows your child, or what they need to thrive, like you do. I don't believe there are any fundamental right or wrong decisions when it comes to education for children – there are only the right or wrong decisions for your child. Whether you choose to delay their entry, start them at school as young as possible or home-educate, what matters most is that you support them through the experience, meeting all their physical, cognitive and emotional needs – the bottom three layers of Maslow's pyramid (see page 11). As parents, you provide the foundations for your child's learning, mindset, happiness and success in life – the ones that will be built upon, whatever education route you choose. Your job is to keep these foundations as secure as possible while your child progresses through their education, ensuring that they are firm right from the very start, when you choose and apply to a school – something we will cover in the following two chapters.

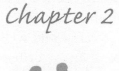

Chapter 2

School Starting Ages, Policies and Procedures

The aim of this chapter is to demystify the application process and policies surrounding it in the four different countries of the United Kingdom.

Here are some of the most common myths:

X You need to put your child's name down for a school place as early as possible, when they're a baby or toddler.

X If you get your application in early, you'll have a better chance of securing a place at your preferred school.

X If you only put one choice on your application, you're more likely to get it.

X You need to write directly to the school you're interested in, so that they know you want a place there.

While there are elements of truth in some of these statements, it depends very much on the type of school you are applying to – state or private – and where in the UK you live. Confusingly, there are a lot of differences between school starting ages, methods and dates for application and place allocations around the UK, due to devolution: in 1997 and 1998, elections were held in Scotland, Wales and Northern Ireland, resulting in the formation of the Scottish Parliament (situated in Edinburgh), the Welsh Assembly (in Cardiff) and the Northern Ireland Assembly (in Belfast), which transferred power for some elements of government from a central base in the UK (Westminster, London) to regional ones in each country. Devolved powers include agriculture, housing and education. Education – and its management – is therefore handled differently in England, Northern Ireland, Scotland and Wales.

State schools

Over 90 per cent of children in the UK attend state schools. Funded by the government, these schools provide an education free of charge. There are several types of state school, and policies and procedures vary according to where you are in the UK.

England

The English school year runs from early September to late July. The compulsory starting age (CSA) for children to begin full-time education in England is five. This includes all children who are five on or before 31 August immediately preceding the new school year in September. However, the standard intake each year includes those who are four years of age on or before 31 August immediately preceding the new school year in September. In other words, unless a parent delays the start of school, English children will begin when they are four years old. In England, children start school in Reception, moving up to Year 1, Year 2 and so on each year.

Deferring starting for summer-born children in England

If your child is 'summer-born' (classified as being born between 1 April and 31 August), you can defer their school place for a year, if you feel that they will not cope well with starting school shortly after their fourth birthday. If this is the case, you need to submit your application at the normal time (i.e. a year before your child is expected to start school at the standard school starting age), and alongside this you should also submit your request to defer their entry until the following year's intake. When you state your intention to defer, it is also important to give detailed reasonings and evidence stating why you not only want to defer your child's entry, but also why you wish them to start in Reception, not Year 1.

Unfortunately, at the time of writing, there is no guarantee that your child will be admitted into a Reception class if you defer their entry; rather, some schools will expect them to start school in Year 1 – technically, the correct age group, based on standard school starting age. It is important to be aware of this when researching and visiting schools. However, the local admissions authority must consider your child's individual needs and whether it would be better for them to start in Reception or Year 1. The consensus among teachers and education experts is that the Reception year is an extremely important one for transitioning children to school and fostering a love of learning, largely through a relaxed and play-based curriculum, and all children, regardless of their age when they start school, should have access to it. Starting school in Year 1 can be a much tougher move for children, as it is more academically focused and less child-friendly. Many parents who delay their summer-born child's entry to school are therefore extremely focused on making sure they start school in a Reception class, not Year 1.

Once you have submitted your application and request, you should be notified of the decision by national offers day, which is in April each year. If your application to defer your child's place (and start in Reception) has been successful, you will then need to withdraw your application and reapply the next year (a ridiculous bureaucratic process, if ever there was one). If your application is not successful, you will be able to refuse the place offered and apply again the following year for a place in Year 1, or you may decide to accept the offer and start your summer-born child in Reception at normal school starting age. If you go with the latter, you do have the option of sending them part-time until the term after their fifth birthday (remembering children do not legally have to receive a full-time education until then), if the school is open to this request for what is known as flexi-schooling.

WHAT DO MOST DO?

Requests for summer-born children to defer school entry and start in Reception a year later, are increasing year on year. The Department for Education's research report into 'Delayed school admissions for summer born pupils' shows that among applications for September 2017, 1,750 requests to delay entry were received, with 75 per cent of these being granted.[1] The following year, 2,243 applications were made to defer entry with a similar success rate. Of local authorities questioned, 11 per cent said they automatically agree to all requests for deferring entry, 63 per cent said they ask parents to make a strong case, but are more open to deferring entry than previously, while 26 per cent said they only allow applications that made a very strong case for deferring entry. The same government report shows that 78 per cent of children whose admissions were delayed were born in either July or August and 15 per cent were born prematurely (compared to the national average prematurity rate of just over 7 per cent), with premature birth being a common reason for a request to defer entry.

English school transport policies

In England, all children aged between five and sixteen years old are eligible for free school transport if they go to their nearest suitable school (usually referred to as their 'catchment' school) and live at least 2 miles away from it for under-eights or at least 3 miles away for over-eights. If there is no safe walking route, then children must be provided with transport to school, regardless of the distance. If you select a school for your child which is *not* the nearest suitable school, then they are not entitled to free school transport.

Free school transport is not an allowance – that is to say, it is not a sum of money paid to parents) and there is generally no choice as to what is provided. In most cases, it will be a school bus collecting and dropping off children close to their homes at the start and end of the school day. If a bus is not viable, then usually a taxi will be provided to and from the child's home, though this is much rarer.

The English application procedure

All state-school applications in England are made directly to your local council, regardless of where the schools are. There is usually no need to tell your chosen school, or schools, that you are applying for a place with them, as all applications are dealt with centrally. The only exception is some faith schools which have their own application form that should be submitted directly to them *in addition to* the council application. If you are considering faith schools, you should contact them for information about their admissions process and policies, as these are set by their own governing bodies.

Your local council should contact you (usually in the autumn, the year before your child is due to start school) with details of how to apply, and the process is usually done online. If, for some reason, you do not receive a letter, you can find details of your local council's application procedure by inputting your postcode on the Government website (see Resources, page 219). Applications open and close on different dates for different councils and they tend to change slightly each year, but they usually open at some point in mid-November (the November of the year before your child is due to start school) and close in mid-January. National offers day – when you are informed of your child's school place allocation – is in mid-April. On this date, if you applied for your child's place online, you will be able to log in to your account to check where your child has been allocated a place. You will also be sent a letter in the post informing you of the outcome of your application.

What if you're not happy with the place you are given?

If you are not allocated a place at your first-choice school, your local council will explain why. Usually, the reason is simply that the school you chose was oversubscribed and you were further down the admissions criteria, most likely because you do not live as close to the school as other families. If you believe that the school's admission code was not followed correctly – for instance, if your child has a special educational need requiring them to attend the school – you may have grounds to appeal. The letter you receive informing you of the outcome of your application will contain details of how to do this. There will be a deadline by which you must appeal (this varies from one authority to the next, but it must be a minimum of twenty school days from the date of the letter you were sent). Your appeal will be heard by an independent panel of three or more people, and will be upheld if the admissions criteria were not followed properly and if they feel your reasons why your child should have been offered a place outweigh those given by the school for not admitting them. Unfortunately, the success rate is quite low, at around 15 per cent.

Whether you appeal or not, you can request to join the waiting list for your preferred school. The same also applies if you were not allocated a place at your second-choice school either. Your child will be given a position on the waiting list, based on their distance from the school. Waiting lists can change often, meaning your child will move up a place if another family does not take up their offer or if they move out of the area; but children can also move down waiting lists if, say, a new family moves to the area who live closer to the school. You will be able to find out where your child is on the waiting list from your local authority, usually from your account on their website.

Wales

The Welsh school year runs from early September to late July. Children living in Wales start school between four and five years of age, depending on how old they are on 1 September, with compulsory attendance beginning at age five (although many will start at four). Children in Wales start school in Reception, moving up to Year 1, Year 2 and so on each subsequent year.

Deferring starting for summer-born children in Wales

The Welsh government's school admissions code does allow parents and carers to request that their child enters school outside the normal year group intake in particular cases.[2] The code states:

> Although most children will be admitted to a school with their own chronological age group, from time to time parents seek places outside their normal age group for gifted and talented children, or those who have experienced problems or missed part of a year, often due to ill health. While it would not normally be appropriate for a child to be placed in a year group that is not concurrent with their chronological age, admission authorities should look at these requests carefully and make decisions on the basis of the circumstances of each case and in consultation with the parents and the school, and specifically in relation to what is most beneficial to the child.

The code also notes that children in Wales do not legally have to be in full-time education until the term after their fifth birthday and that parents and carers can request that a child who is younger than this goes to school part-time, or defers entry until later in the school year. Unfortunately, though, there is less legal standing for this in Wales than in other parts of the UK.

English- or Welsh-speaking?

The Welsh government is keen for children to speak Welsh as well as English, and it is therefore taught as part of the national curriculum. Schools may communicate with children and teach all lessons in Welsh during the foundation stage (these are known as Welsh-medium schools) or only some (known as English-medium schools), and schools are not legally required to teach English in Years 1 and 2. The amount of Welsh communicated and spoken in English-mediums differs between schools. Around a quarter of Welsh schools are Welsh-mediums. Some schools operate a dual-stream process, whereby some children are taught in a Welsh and others in English.

Why choose a Welsh-medium school?

Welsh-medium schools carry the significant benefit of raising children to be bilingual, fostering competence in Welsh as well as English. Being bilingual carries many advantages for children, including having better attention, better adjustment to environmental change, better cognitive processing and finding other languages easier to learn later in life.[3] Alongside this, the emphasis on learning and speaking Welsh can foster a sense of pride in Welsh culture and heritage (or in the place that they live, if they do not come from a Welsh family).

Schooling in Welsh does not mean that children are not proficient in English. In fact, they become competent in both languages, with children attending Welsh-medium schools reaching the same standards of English as those at English-mediums by the end of their primary-school education. Similarly, if you do not speak Welsh at home, this will not hinder your child at school at all, and communication to parents and homework instructions will usually be provided in both English and Welsh. It is also not a prerequisite for children attending a Welsh-medium school to speak Welsh before they start. Finally, some children come from families where neither Welsh, nor English is the main language at home, and this does not present a barrier to attending a Welsh-medium.

For some parents it is not important that their child learns the Welsh language – perhaps because they are not Welsh speakers themselves, they live in an area with a very low percentage of Welsh speakers or they believe that their children will not need to use the language as they grow up. Where parents aren't Welsh speakers, they can sometimes be concerned, as mentioned, about communication with the school and helping their child with work, including homework. Sometimes attending a Welsh-medium school means travelling out of the immediate neighbourhood and parents feel that their child not attending a local school is a significant downside. Or sometimes there is simply not one near enough to make travel feasible.

According to research findings, Welsh-mediums offer many benefits and no risks; however, finding the right fit for your child will mean taking many different factors and variables into consideration, and the option of a Welsh-medium may or may not be a priority for you.

Welsh school transport policies

Welsh local authorities must provide free transport to and from school if a primary-aged child lives 2 or more miles away and is attending their nearest suitable school. To be classed as 'suitable', a school should meet all the needs (educational and physical) of the attending child. If a parent chooses to send their child to a school that is not the closest suitable one, then they are not entitled to free school transport. If the child lives less than 2 miles from school, but there is no suitable walking route available, then transport should also be provided.

The Welsh application procedure

Welsh school applications are made directly to the local authority, usually via their online system, unless you are applying for a faith school, in which case you often need to apply directly to the school too. As in England, applications usually open at some point in mid-November (the November in the year before your child is due to start school) and close in mid-January. National offers day, when you are informed of your child's school place allocation, is in mid-April. If you applied for your child's place online you will be sent an email advising you of their allocated place; if you applied on paper, you will be sent a letter in the post.

What if you're not happy with the place you are given?

If you are not happy with the school your child has been offered, you can appeal. You must do this by the end of May by contacting your local council in writing – either by post or email (the precise details will be outlined in the offer letter you receive). You have grounds for appeal if the admissions criteria of the school you applied for have not been followed properly or they are not considered legal. If either of these is found to be the case, then you will be awarded a place at the school. Finally, you can also appeal if the decision to refuse your child a place is not reasonable. This is harder to prove, and you will need to submit evidence to back your argument; however, the appeal panel may decide that your reasons why your child should attend the school outweigh those for which the place was declined. In Wales, fewer than 5 per cent of appeals for primary places are successful.

If your appeal is not successful, you can still ask to be put on a waiting list for another school, or schools. Your child will move up or down the waiting list, depending on other people declining their places and families moving out of or into the area.

Scotland

The Scottish school year starts in mid-August and runs until late June. Children start school in P1 (Primary One), moving up to P2, P3 and so on each subsequent year. The school starting age for any given year includes children born between the beginning of the March immediately preceding school entry (those who are already five when they start) to those who have had their birthday by the end of the February after they start (those who are four when they start). This means that children are aged between four and a half and five and a half when they start school in Scotland, unless a parent delays their start.

Deferring starting for autumn- and winter-born children in Scotland

If your child was born in January or February, you will be able to defer their school start to the following August (meaning that they will be five and a half years old when they start school) if you wish. If your child was born between September and December, you will be able to request to defer starting school for another year (meaning that they will be almost six when they start school), although this is not automatically granted (as it is for those born in January or February). Instead, requests must be approved by your local education authority. If your child was born in January or February and you defer their start for another year, then they are entitled to another year's preschool funding. Unfortunately, even if you do manage to defer entry for a September–December-born child, they are not eligible for another year of preschool funding.

Findings from the 'Growing up in Scotland: Early Experiences of Primary School' report indicate:[4]

- When they started school, 42 per cent of children were under five, 49 per cent were aged between five and five and a half and 9 per cent were older than five and a half.

- Eighty-seven per cent of children who started school in the August were of standard school start age (between four and a half and five and a half) and 13 per cent were deferred to the following year.

- Of the 13 per cent of children whose places were deferred, 53 per cent were automatic deferrals (children born in January or February) and 47 per cent were deferral requests (born between September and December).

- It is more common for parents of boys to defer their school start, with 15 per cent of boys versus 9 per cent of girls deferred.

Is it possible to start school earlier in Scotland?

If you want your child to start school before the standard school start age (when they are only just four years old), then contact your council and explain the reasons behind your request. There is no statutory right for parents to ask this, but if the council agree with your reasons, they will provide your child with a P1 place in a school. You can request a specific school, but you cannot appeal if you are not given a place there.

English- or Scottish-speaking?

As with Wales, some (but not all) Scottish local authorities offer Gaelic-medium education. Again, the initial focus is on children learning Gaelic to build on fluency, usually with the whole curriculum being taught in Gaelic during the primary-school years. Some schools also offer both Gaelic- and English-medium education. The benefits here are identical to those of Welsh-medium schools (see page 43), with no discernible downsides from a research perspective, but personal belief and choice for each individual family are obviously important too.

Scottish school transport policy

If your child lives more than 2 miles from their designated school, then the council is responsible for providing transport to and from school. If you select a school that is not the designated one, then the council does not have to provide transport, regardless of distance. They may be willing to help, but there is no legal obligation for them to do so.

The Scottish application procedure

If you are happy with the school assigned to you by your local council, then all you need to do is to enrol by the designated date. If you would prefer a different school from the one you've been allocated (or are likely to be allocated), you must tell the council (usually within a specified time limit). You should put this request in writing, including your name and address, your child's name, date of birth and the name of the school you would prefer. If you are applying for more than one school, you must indicate your first choice. If you are applying for a school that is not your designated one and you submit your request by 15 March, then the council must let you know their decision by

30 April of the same year. If your child is of school starting age, you will usually receive information from your local council in the December, January or February before the August they will start school. If you have not received anything by late February, then get in touch with the council or school you are interested in and check the date by which you need to put in your request. If you are certain of your school choice at this point, then the earlier you submit your request the better.

What if you're not happy with the place you are given?

If your council cannot provide a place in the school you request, they must give you their reason in writing. If you disagree with this, your first step is to approach the person who wrote the letter and request more information. If you are still not happy after this, then you can approach an appeals committee. This must be done no later than twenty-eight days after receiving notification that your child has not received a place at your chosen school. You can only appeal once per school year, so if you have a second-choice school you would be happy with, it may be better to request a place there before appealing your first-choice school. The letter you receive from your council will provide details of how to appeal.

Northern Ireland

Northern Ireland is the only country in the UK where four-year-olds are legally obliged to attend school. Children in Northern Ireland start school depending on their age on 1 July immediately preceding the start of the new school year. If they are four years old between 1 September and 1 July the following year, they will start the new school year in the September following their fourth birthday. If they turn four between 2 July and 31 August, they will start school the following September, after their fifth birthday. There is currently no legislative provision in place for deferral for those children born in April, May and June, or on 1 July. At the time of writing, however, there are campaigns running to try to address this.

Upon starting school in Northern Ireland, children enter in Year 1, rather than Reception.

Northern Irish school transport policy

Children in Northern Ireland are entitled to free school transport if there is no suitable school within the statutory qualifying distance of their home and they are of compulsory school age. For children under eleven years of age the statutory qualifying distance is 2 miles.

The Northern Irish application procedure

The Education Authority manages almost all state-school applications in Northern Ireland, although there is a slightly different process for those applying for a place for a child with special educational needs. Admissions criteria are decided by the Board of Governors, or Management Committee in each individual school and children are admitted based upon these criteria. Applications for a state-school place are made online, via the Parent Portal, on the Education Authority's website (see Resources, page 219). Applications must be made between 2 and 31 January, and you will be asked to list your four preferred schools. Supplementary information and documentation may be requested, and you will be asked to present your child's birth certificate directly to your first choice of school no later than one week after the application closing date.

What if you're not happy with the place you are given?

If your child is not given a place at your preferred school and you are concerned that the school's admission criteria were not followed, then you may argue the decision with an independent appeals panel. This panel will decide if the school has correctly applied their admissions criteria; if they have not done so, then your child will be offered a place. You should contact the Education Authority in your area to appeal – details of how to do so will be given in your offer letter.

Private (Fee-paying) schools

This chapter has so far focused on state (free) schooling. But what about private schools? These have their own admissions policies, and depending on your location and the schools that you are interested in, you may find that they prefer you to send your child from the age of three to their pre-preparatory (commonly called pre-prep) or nursery section. However, compulsory school starting age still applies, and you should not feel pressured into sending your child earlier than you would like to, just to secure a place at a school.

Private schools all have a deadline by which you should apply for your child's place. This tends to fall broadly in line with application dates for state schools, but you should always check those that you are interested in to make sure. It is possible that your child may be assessed when you apply for a private- or fee-paying-school place, even for one in Reception, if the school is particularly academic. At this age, assessment usually focuses on looking at communication skills, although it may include other aspects. Most schools will also require you to pay a registration deposit and it is unlikely that you will receive a refund on this should you decide to turn down any place offered. This is something to strongly consider if you are applying to two, three or more schools.

If your child is offered a place in your chosen school, you will receive a letter of acceptance. You will be given a short period of time (usually two to four weeks) in which to formally accept the place and pay a deposit or a term's fees in advance. This payment will secure your child's place and forms part of a legally binding contract. If you do not subsequently take up the place it is likely that your payment will be non-refundable.

No matter where you live, or whether you are hoping for your child to attend a state or private school, you will still need to visit some schools and ask many questions before making any decisions. The next chapter will help you to know what to look for in a good school and what questions to ask in order to ensure that you are making the best possible choices for your child.

Chapter 3

Choosing a School

When I was choosing a school for my firstborn, I had no idea that there were so many different types. I naïvely thought that the choice would simply be between state (free) and private (fee-paying). In my research, I came across many different terms and acronyms that left me feeling confused. What was an 'aided' school or a 'voluntary-controlled' one, for example? And what was a free school (not so called because you don't have to pay) or an academy? It felt like I needed to go to school just to learn about my child going to school.

This chapter will give you the confidence you need when making the choice of a school for your child. It will help you to understand what you should look for, what questions to ask when you visit, how to make sense of official reports and how to make sure that the school you choose is a good fit for both your child and yourself.

Different types of school

To make your choice confidently, you will need to understand about the different types of school in the UK and the terminology that goes with them. The five main ones are as follows:

1. **State-maintained (including faith schools)** State-maintained schools make up the largest percentage of UK schools. They are free to attend and are overseen and paid for by the local authority. State-maintained schools must be 'all ability', which means they must not select pupils based upon academic competence and achievement.

   They are subdivided into four main categories:

   • **Voluntary-aided** These are part-funded by a religious organisation or trust. The land or buildings may also be owned by the same organisation. They are run by the governing body – this is a group of governors made up of parents, staff and members of the religious organisation or trust and local authority.

   • **Voluntary-controlled** These are the same as voluntary-aided schools, with the exception that they are controlled by the local authority.

   • **Community** These are controlled by the local authority.

   • **Foundation and trust** These are run by the governing body of the school.

   State-maintained schools must follow the National Curriculum, but faith schools (voluntary-aided or voluntary-controlled) have more freedom to choose their own religious-education teaching. Faith schools fall into a further two categories, these being denominational (one specific religion) or non-denominational (not restricted to one specific religion). Faith schools can prioritise admissions for up to 50 per cent of pupils based on their religious faith. They account for around a quarter of all UK schools (most either being Church of England or Roman Catholic) and they tend to outperform non-faith schools.

2. **Free schools** Free schools are non-profit making, independent state schools that are funded by the government. They are not controlled by the local authority. Instead, they have a 'funding agreement' – a type of legally binding contract, which means they are held accountable to the government. The first free schools came into being in 2011, after the Academies Act of 2010. The aim was for them to drive up standards in education, but they have frequently come under fire for not delivering quite what was hoped for in terms of saving money. Nevertheless, the government continues to invest in the creation of more free schools and some perform exceptionally well, with more of them being rated as 'Outstanding' than maintained schools.

   Free schools can be set up by a variety of people and groups, including parents, teachers, businesses, religious organisations and groups and charities. They do not have to follow the National Curriculum, but they must provide a 'broad and balanced' curriculum that includes the core subjects of maths, English and science. They must also be 'all ability'.

3. **Academies** Academies are independent schools funded with money received directly from the government. This

means that they are free for pupils to attend, but are not funded by the local council, like state-maintained schools. Academies were introduced as part of the same 2010 initiative that created free schools. An academy can be created when the school performs below the expected national average, thus allowing it much more of an opportunity to improve, or schools can simply choose to become one (known as 'converters'). Academies are given more freedom to choose their own curriculum, but must cover core subjects such as maths, English and science and must also teach religious education.

Academies are often run as part of a multi-academy trust (MAT), where fellow academy schools work together to create one larger organisation and can share in best practices. Academies must be 'all ability'.

4. **Independent, private or fee-paying schools** Independent schools receive no funding from the government and are free of state and local-authority control. Instead, they are funded by fees paid by parents of children who attend, fundraising, sponsorship, gifts and bequests. Many private schools offer scholarships, fee reductions and means-tested bursaries for those on a lower income, particularly if children exhibit any special gifts or talents in sport or the arts. Fees for independent schools are usually charged termly, the average fee being around £5,000 to £6,000 per term for day pupils (non-boarders).

Private schools are free to select students based on their ability and some may set entrance tests and exams, although these are not common at the early-years level (age four to seven). They are also not required to follow the national curriculum, although they should provide a broad education, including core subjects such as English, maths and science. Schools are free to select which tests and qualifications students sit for. While there are no mandatory state inspections, some are inspected by OFSTED and others by the Independent Schools Inspectorate. The other main difference between these and state schools is that independent schools are not legally obliged to appoint teachers with qualified teacher status (QTS). Some independent schools may offer a traditional academic education, while others provide a more alternative one, including those based upon Montessori, Democratic or Steiner pedagogies.

Rather than organising classes based upon Infant, Junior and Senior divisions, independent schools tend to be arranged as follows:

- Pre-preparatory (or pre-prep): from age four to seven

- Preparatory (or prep): from age eight to eleven or thirteen

- Senior: from age eleven or thirteen through to eighteen
  Some independent schools will offer all stages from four to eighteen years, whereas others may offer just one, for example, a dedicated pre-prep school. Some parents will send their child to an independent school with a view to them staying there from pre-prep all the way through to the end of senior school, whereas others will move their children to different schools for each stage, even if more than one stage is offered. Similarly, some prefer to use a mix of both independent and state schooling, choosing an independent pre-prep and then a state junior and senior school, for example.

5. **Special schools** Special schools are for those who have special educational needs and disabilities (SEND) which would not be well catered for in a mainstream school

(although some mainstream schools also have a SEND unit attached to them). Usually children attending are in receipt of an Education, Health and Care Plan (EHC) – the result of a special investigation and assessment into the needs of the child and the type of education and care that they need.

Special schools are usually maintained by the local authority, but independent (both fee-paying and free) special schools do exist. Staff will have special SEND training, and facilities will cater specifically to the children and their needs (special education provision or SEP). The pupil-to-staff ratio is usually much lower than it is for mainstream schools. Maintained special schools follow the National Curriculum; however, it will be adapted to suit the abilities of the children attending. Independent special schools do not need to follow the National Curriculum. Some special schools will focus on a specific type of need, such as communication and interaction, whereas others will focus broadly on all needs.

The pros and cons of independent schools

I am lucky enough to live in an area with excellent state schools that meet my children's needs. There is nothing a local independent school could offer that we can't get for free. If I lived elsewhere, though, it might be different. Provisions aside, my preference would always be for my children to attend a state school because I like the idea that they are socialising with children from all walks of life and I am not keen on the social segregation that can come with independent schools, although

I do appreciate that they take some of the pressure off the state education system financially.

Making the choice between independent and state schooling is hugely personal, taking not only your family's finances and ideologies into account, but also the options available to you locally, as well as your child's own individual strengths and needs and where these would be better met. The other point to be aware of is that not all independent schools are created equally – as with state schools, there are some brilliant ones and some not-so-good ones. Again, considering what they offer individually is key. The table below contains some of the pros and cons of independent schooling:

Pros	Cons
More likely to get a place at the school of your choosing, especially if it is not very close to your home.	Places at the best schools can be very competitive and go quickly. You may need to apply several years before your child is due to start and your child may need to sit an entrance test.
Higher academic achievement; most of the top-performing schools in the UK are independents.	May not suit students who are less academic and especially those with special educational needs.
The reputation of the school attended might help the child with future education and career prospects.	Lack of opportunity to mix with children from different cultural and social demographics.
Not subjected to standard government inspections and assessments (and therefore not teaching to achieve good scores in them).	Potential for substandard teaching to fall through the net in the absence of government inspection.

Do not have to teach to the National Curriculum; free to choose syllabus to best suit children.	May not focus on the areas that your child would excel in, for instance music or art.
Usually smaller class sizes.	Can make it harder for children to make like-minded friends if class sizes are too small.
Experienced and enthusiastic staff and alternative education options possibly available, for example, Montessori and Steiner teaching.	Teachers are not necessarily required to have qualified teacher status.
Independent schools save the government money, allowing more to be spent on those who cannot afford independent schools.	Expensive fees and the need to make sure you can afford them not just now, but in the future, for the duration of the child's schooling.
Potential to have better facilities, especially with sports, technology and arts provision.	Some independent schools struggle with finances and facilities need updating.
Possibility of single-sex schooling, even at infant and junior stage.	Many children will thrive more in a co-educational school setting.
Potential for boarding at a later age, should you move away and want to maintain continuity for your child.	Some children will really find boarding and separation from parents difficult, which can have a long-lasting negative impact.

State school – do you *really* have a choice?

How much of a choice do you have when it comes to applying for a school place? There is no simple answer here, sadly. It comes down to geography – where you live in relation to your preferred school – and how many others are applying for a place in the same school. It is therefore probably more accurate to refer to preferences here, rather than choices – because while you can absolutely indicate your preference in your application, and you may be lucky enough to be given a place at your preferred school, it is not something that is within your control.

Most schools will prioritise those children who live closest to the school (often termed 'in catchment') and those with siblings already there. Those children who are adopted or looked after (fostered) or who have SEND which are met by the school will usually also sit at the top of the entrance criteria. So if you are applying for a school that you have no familial link to and you live quite a distance away, the chances of getting a place there are much lower than if you apply for one that's a stone's throw from your home or one that an older child already attends. That isn't to say that there is no chance of getting a place at a school that is not your catchment one. Again, it depends entirely on how many others apply for it, where they live and if they have siblings there. Schools may be able to tell you whether they are expecting a high or low sibling intake if you ask them in advance of applying. Similarly, investigating the birth rate of the year that your child was born can give you an indication of whether it is a high or low birth-rate year (whether the number of children born in the same year as your child was higher or lower than average). You will obviously have a greater chance of getting a place, particularly out of catchment, if it is a low birth-rate year.

The graph overleaf illustrates birth rates in the UK from 2012 to 2017 (the numbers shown are live births per thousand women).[1] Based upon this, 2017 would be counted as a low birth-rate year, at 11.4 births per thousand women, whereas 2012 would be high, at 12.8 births per thousand women. The Office for National Statistics release birth-rate data each year, for the two previous years.

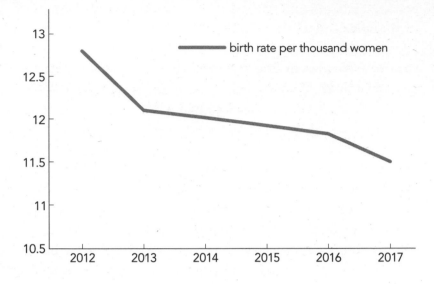

In the UK, around 85 per cent of families will be granted a place at their first-choice state school, although this obviously varies based upon the birth rate, the number of siblings applying for a place, proximity to your chosen school and its popularity.

Major influences in making a decision

If you think back to your early school days, what are your fondest memories? For most people it's about their friends or playing outside – a sense of belonging and fun that is crucial to a child's happiness and success at school. Ultimately, you want to choose a school that will meet as many levels of Maslow's pyramid as possible (see page 11). While friendship and social interaction are key, they need to be combined with some of the more practical elements on the following pages.

Practical considerations

The following are points you may wish to think about from a practical point of view:

Proximity to home

The distance from your home to school impacts not only on the likelihood of your child gaining a place, but also on the structure of every single day that they attend the school, potentially your finances, the environment and your child's friendships. A long commute means early starts in the morning – a time of day that can already bring a lot of tension when you're trying to get a child out of the door. It is also means getting home later in the day, and long journeys with tired children can be stressful. If you are not entitled to free school transport (see page 39), you will also need to factor in the cost of transportation, whether that is bus fares or car fuel. It's good to have an idea of how much this will add up to over a year and to compare this figure for different schools. From an environmental-impact perspective, a school that can be reached by foot or bike is something to consider. And don't forget that you won't just be commuting to the area the school is in for school attendance – there is a big social side to school too. Living locally will make it easier to arrange playdates and get to after-school and weekend school activities (such as plays, parents' evenings, fetes and birthday parties).

Feeding from current preschool/nursery

Some preschools and nurseries act as official feeders for certain schools, which may impact on your child gaining a place. Others have no official connection, although many children attending will attend one specific school, meaning that your child will know most of those starting school with them. If a preschool or nursery is situated in school grounds, children will likely already be very familiar with the school, which can make settling in much easier. This was the case for all my children, and the familiarity with the school from their nursery years made the transition so much easier for them all. However, it is no bad thing to send your child to a different school. Although they may not know any other children there and it may be unfamiliar, you must look at all your child's needs and how the school meets them. If you feel the school attached to preschool or nursery is a good fit, then it seems an obvious choice, but if you aren't so keen on it, don't be afraid to go elsewhere. Children make friends very easily at this age and not knowing any other children at the new school really shouldn't be a stumbling block. Similarly, most children are very flexible and adapt quickly to new settings.

Feeder schools for a specific secondary

Time goes by insanely quickly when you have children, and sooner than you know it you will be thinking about secondary-school places. Giving a little thought to any potential impact on this now will be something you will thank yourself for in six or seven years' time. What secondary school does a primary feed into? Will it have any influence on the chances of your child being allocated a place at a well-regarded secondary? If you already have a particular secondary in mind, call them and ask them which primary schools feed into theirs, or ask the infant school where most of the children end up going to secondary. Yes, it is confusing having to consider not one, but two, school choices, but thinking about this now really can make things easier for your family in the future.

Places for younger siblings

If you have more than one child, or you hope to have another baby in the future, you will need to factor in the chances of any younger siblings getting a place in your chosen school. If it is a low birth-rate year and you choose a school out of your local catchment area, you may get a place for your oldest child, but end up having to juggle two different school runs if your younger child (or children) does not get allocated a place at the same school. Most schools take into account siblings already at the school when you are applying for a school place, pushing applications for younger siblings to the top of their entry criteria, but this rule may only apply if you live in catchment. If you live out of catchment, you may find yourself a long way down the admissions criteria, behind those in catchment (both with and without siblings). How will you manage school runs and events if your children end up at different schools?

Availability of wraparound care

If you work outside the home, the chances are that before- and after-school childcare will be important to you. Find out if the school you are looking at offers a breakfast club and after-school club (termed 'wraparound care') on site, or if your child will have to be transported to and from school from elsewhere. How much does the wraparound care cost? What time do they open in the morning? What's the latest time you can collect in the evening? Do they provide care during school holidays? These are all important questions. And how do you feel about the provider of the wraparound care – are you happy with them? After all, your child may end up spending up to three or four hours per day there, so it should be something that you feel suits you and your child well.

SEND/pastoral support

If your child has any SEND, then this should be at the top of your list of requirements. How will the school meet your child's special needs? What is their reputation for SEND support? Here, it can help to speak to parents in local support groups, to understand the school's approaches and find the best one for your child's needs. Also, consider the pastoral support; this is help for children who, for whatever reason, may struggle at school. Good pastoral care is so important. Ask the school what they offer for children who grapple with tricky behaviour, friendship issues, anxiety and so on. A reliable sign of a great school versus a not-so-good one is how they regard and care for their pupils' mental health.

Availability of and access to outdoor spaces

Young children thrive when they spend time outside. They need to run, jump, climb and roll in natural settings. What opportunities for outdoor play and learning does the school you are looking at offer? Do they have a grassed play area, as well as a concrete or tarmac one? Do they have an outdoor classroom? Do they offer a Forest School programme (hands-on learning in a woodland or other natural setting)? Do the children have plenty of opportunities to go outside during the school day? These are all important considerations, especially if you have a free-spirited child who loves to move.

Art, music, drama and sports provision

Schools are increasingly under pressure from government to focus more on so-called academic subjects, like reading, writing and maths. Although the early years are very focused on play, the latter years at school can be very desk-bound. This lack of creativity and movement can make school very hard for children, especially those who are not thought of as academically gifted. Remember – when you choose a school, its' not just for a couple of years, so looking at the opportunities for the arts and sports as your child grows is so important. What provisions and facilities are there for nine-, ten- and eleven-year olds to draw, paint, sculpt, sing, dance, act, run and swim? Are the arts and sports relegated mostly to lunch and after-school clubs or does the school incorporate them into the everyday curriculum?

Clubs and after-school activities

School clubs and activities help to make the school day more holistic. They give children an opportunity to learn new skills that cannot be focused on during the normal school day – for instance, cookery, gardening, sewing, learning an instrument and team sports. Sadly, with governmental spending cuts, most schools can't afford to provide these activities for free and they usually come at a cost for most parents. However, are they provided at all? Is there a wide variety of activities and clubs on offer? Is there something that will interest your child? These are all things that you should look into.

Percentage of male and female teachers

Chapter 1 touched on the impact of the lack of male teachers at school. While the effect on children may be small, a school which actively seeks to recruit male teachers can be indicative of a more forward-thinking, less gender-biased environment. If you have a preference for a male teacher for your child, this may be something to consider, but bear in mind that teachers can and do leave and classes don't necessarily have the same teacher each year.

Class and school size

Class size can impact not only on a child's academic achievement at school, but also their friendships and happiness. The positive effects of class sizes are seen in a class of fewer than twenty pupils, with negative effects mostly seen in a class of over thirty-five; the impact between twenty and thirty-five pupils is not as significant (see also page 19). Remember though, that fewer children in the class can present fewer friendship opportunities for children, especially those of the same sex. When my daughter started school, she was one of only five girls in her class of nineteen boys. This caused quite a bit of friction for several years for the girls, with the constant falling out and making up that tends to happen. The whole school size is something to think about too. Do you think your child will thrive in a small, village-like school or do they need the stimulation and hustle and bustle of a large, busy one, where there are lots of children to socialise and interact with.

Summer-born/flexi-schooling policies

If you have a summer-born child, understanding the school's approach to delayed entry and flexi-school is important. Are they happy for children who are held back a year to start in Reception, rather than skipping straight to Year 1 (see page 26)? What are their views on flexi-schooling? For instance, would they be happy for your child to start part-time, for mornings only, or to attend for only two or three days per week, until they reach compulsory school age?

Settling-in procedures

The settling-in procedure can give a good insight into a school's ethos. Consider whether the school you are looking at offers taster days or sessions at the end of the school year before your child begins there, to familiarise them with things. Do they allow children to attend part-time initially? If so, how long can they attend part-time before they are expected to go full-time? And is there any provision for children who are ready to start full-time from the off?

Communication with parents

Your relationship with your child's school and any communication you have with them are important factors in your child's future happiness and success there. Look at the following: how the school keeps in touch with parents; whether there is a weekly newsletter and a parent-only section on their web site; if there are regular parents' evenings; how the new and growing technology is used to allow parents to view details of their child's day online and share information with teachers; whether the school encourages parents to go in to help with reading or get involved with the running of clubs and so on; if parental feedback is regularly requested; if staff have an open-door policy; and how approachable any governors are.

Parent–teacher association

Parent–teacher associations (or PTAs) are groups of parents, teachers and other school staff who meet and form a committee whose primary aim is to support the school, usually through fundraising. PTAs often raise money for library, play, IT, sporting and other equipment and tend to hold many different events throughout the year, such as school fetes, non-uniform days, school discos and the like. The presence of an active PTA is a good indicator of involved parents and staff who are passionate about improving the school.

Behaviour policies

Understanding what a school expects in terms of behaviour and how they manage it can give you a good insight into their beliefs and ethos. All schools will have a discipline policy, which you can usually access on their website. If you cannot find it, contact the school and ask them to send you one to review.

Look at how they manage difficult behaviour. Do they favour a behaviourist carrot-and-stick approach (rewards and punishments) or do they adopt a more modern relationship-and-attachment-style approach, focusing on the connection between staff and pupils and considering the emotional needs of children? The latter is not only more effective and age appropriate, but much gentler and kinder on children. Unfortunately, most schools tend to adopt a behaviourist approach, with stickers, rewards, house points and certificates sitting in the carrot category and exclusion of some form sitting in the punishment category. If this seems to apply to the school you are interested in, find out exactly how they implement their policy and ask what their beliefs are surrounding age-appropriate behaviour and unmet needs. Do they tend to blame the child for their difficult behaviour and expect them or their parents to fix the problem? Or do they take a more collaborative approach to helping the child to feel happier at school, thus resulting in better behaviour? How flexible are they in their approach to discipline? How do they take feedback? And finally, how do you think your child will cope with these policies?

Many parents worry about behaviourist discipline policies and yet have children who will rarely require school discipline. These children tend to thrive despite the school's policy. Others, though, particularly those with SEND, can really suffer at the hands of a school with a behaviourist discipline policy.

I have a child with ADHD and the very traditional and inflexible carrot-and-stick approach at his school was quite toxic and unhelpful for him. Looking at your individual child here is as important, if not more so, than just the behaviour policy. Many parents are unnecessarily scared by school discipline and others do not pay enough attention to it.

Emotional considerations

Now let's look at the more emotional side of things when you are choosing a school.

Opinions of current parents and students

Nothing can give you more of an insight into a school than speaking to those who currently attend it and their caregivers. If you know anybody with children at the school in question, ask what they think of it. What do they think are the best parts of the school and what are they unhappy with, or feel needs improvement? If you can speak to the children, then even better. If you don't know anyone personally, then perhaps walk past at the end of the school day and chat to those on the school run, or join a local parenting group on social media and ask on there.

Family ties and links

For some parents, it is important for their children to go to the same school that they did as a child or the same one as other family members. While personal knowledge of the school from your own childhood gives some insight, you should remember that a lot might have changed in the decades since you left. Only the buildings tend to remain the same. Also, what suited you won't necessarily suit your child. However, family members attending the school at the same time – for instance, cousins – can be helpful when it comes to settling your child in and for providing someone to share school runs with. Plus, you can get great current insider information.

Your intuition

Have you ever looked around a house or flat and just known it was right for you? Maybe you couldn't put your finger on why, but even though it did not fulfil all your requirements, you just knew it was 'the one'. When it comes to the right school for your child, this sort of intuition can be very strong. You may get a strong feeling that a school is a good fit, even when a lot of boxes remain unticked, or there are practical things about it that don't quite measure up. Try not to let your rational brain get in the way too much here and trust your gut; it won't let you – or your child – down.

Your child's preference

Take your child with you when you visit schools and ask them which they prefer and what they like (and dislike) about each of the them. If school open days are for adults only, ask if you can visit again at another time with your child. They will be attending the school for many years, so they should get a say, although some of their reasons should be taken more lightly than others. For instance, 'I like that school because it has a big picture of a dinosaur' should not carry the same weight as 'that school made me feel very scared/sad'. Also, look at your child's general demeanour when you visit; you can often tell a lot from how they behave, which can be more revealing than what they tell you verbally.

Some schools can tick every box in the practical considerations, yet leave your heart feeling empty, whereas others can feel instinctively right, despite barriers or less than ideal practical provisions. In my experience, the emotional concerns are always the most important ones when choosing infant and junior schools.

Understanding official reports and scores

Official school inspectorate and assessment bodies – namely, OFSTED in England, Estyn in Wales, Education Scotland and the Education and Training Inspectorate in Northern Ireland – all produce reports and scores for individual schools.

Inspection reports can be helpful when choosing a school, but they should not be viewed in isolation. Each of them comes with its own flaws, including the fact that schools may teach in such a way as to specifically get a good inspection outcome – 'gaming the system' – which is not necessarily in the children's best interests. They are also limited in what they can measure. For instance, they cannot tell you about the emotional wellbeing and happiness of individual children, nor can they tell you if the school is a good fit for your child. Some reports may also be quite out of date and not present the true current picture of the school, which is why you should always take into account the date of the last inspection when reading reports. This is especially true of those in receipt of an 'outstanding' rating from OFSTED, which means they are currently exempt from any future routine inspections. A so-called outstanding school could therefore go uninspected for many years, during which time it may no longer be outstanding, but in the absence of a routine inspection that rating still stands.

When choosing schools for my own children, I largely

disregarded the OFSTED reports. In fact, we chose a school which OFSTED said 'requires improvement', because it felt nurturing and holistic, as opposed to the good- and outstanding-rated schools which felt too impersonal and academic.

However, official inspections are not solely designed to inform parents or provide a rating for schools – they also provide feedback to headteachers and other staff about ways in which the school can be improved, as well as identifying those that are in urgent need of immediate attention. When reading reports, it is important to keep this in mind, as although areas identified for improvement can seem like a negative, they can actually be viewed as a positive because the head and other teachers will be working on them.

Here is a guide to the overall ratings and what they mean:

OFSTED

- **Outstanding** These schools are said to provide an exceptionally good education for all attending.

- **Good** These schools are considered to provide a solid and satisfactory education for those attending, with a few small areas of improvement still needing attention.

- **Requires improvement** These schools are deemed neither inadequate nor satisfactory. Work is needed to improve certain areas.

- **Inadequate** These schools are considered to have significant weaknesses and, as such, are not providing an appropriate education for those attending. Urgent remedial work is needed.

Estyn

- **Excellent** Defined as, 'Very strong, sustained performance and practice'.

- **Good** Defined as, 'Strong features, although minor aspects may require improvement'.

- **Adequate and needs improvement** Defined as, 'Strengths outweigh weaknesses, but important aspects require improvement'.

- **Unsatisfactory and needs urgent improvement** Defined as, 'Important weaknesses outweigh strengths'.

Education Scotland

Schools in Scotland are not scored with official grades. Instead, inspectors produce a document detailing the strengths and weaknesses of the school and indicating any targets and improvements it should work towards.

Education and Training Inspectorate

The Northern Irish system is very similar to that of England and Wales, aside from providing a few more categories as follows:

- Outstanding
- Very Good
- Good

- Satisfactory

- Inadequate

- Unsatisfactory

League tables

As well as reading formal reports, you may also wish to look at school league tables which you can find online or published annually in national newspapers. These are based on the results of standard attainment tests (SATs, taken in Year 6), which measure performance in specific academic areas, including reading, writing, mathematics and science. Schools that perform better at SATs will appear higher up the league tables, although the tests have been widely criticised, not just because of the stress that they cause to children sitting them, but because they provide a very limited picture of a school's performance. They don't take into account emotional wellbeing, happiness, social skills, drive to learn, achievement in the arts or sport; rather, they provide a snapshot of how a school teaches to the tests and an indication of the demographics of a school. For instance, schools with a higher proportion of children with SEND will score lower in SATs and appear further down the league tables, as will those with a higher proportion of children for whom English is their second language. League tables tell you very little about everyday life at a school, or how well it prepares its children for future learning.

Planning school visits

While official reports, statistics and websites can help to give you an objective view of a school, there is no substitute for visiting and speaking to staff and pupils in real life. School visits should be one of the most important parts of your preparation and, ultimately, your choice of school.

Schools tend to hold open days in the autumn, a couple of months before applications are due in. They will often advertise these in local newspapers and on their websites. It is up to you to find out when they are being held. Almost all will take place on a weekday, during school hours, so if you work, it is worth contacting schools that you are interested in as soon as possible, to find out when their open days take place and book time off work if you can. They will usually know the date several months before it is advertised.

What to look for or ask at an open day

Tours of the school are often run by the most senior pupils. This can be off-putting to parents initially, who may prefer to be shown around by a staff member, but it is actually a unique opportunity to find out about the school from some of the most important people – the pupils themselves. Children tend to be brutally honest, whereas staff members will be more diplomatic. Ask them questions and make full use of the opportunity. On your tour, you should also ask to see lesser-covered areas, such as the changing rooms or pupils' toilets – the condition of these can give you a good indication of the school's outlook. For instance, pupils' toilets that are well kept (although they may be old) and brightly painted to appeal to children are usually the sign of a caring school

A good open day will also give you an opportunity to speak to the headteacher and other staff. Better still, you might get to view a lesson in progress. If so, really observe how the teachers interact with the children and how the children respond. What the staff say and do with the children is of far more importance than what they say to you.

Here are some useful questions you may want to ask the teachers and/or children at an open day:

- Do you enjoy working/going here?

- What are you most proud of about your school?

- What do you think the school could be better at?

- Do you have any plans to improve certain things in the future?

- What is the biggest challenge your school is facing at the moment?

- How do you cope with difficult or unwanted behaviour from children?

- What is your view on rewarding children for good behaviour, or for attendance?

- What is your view on starting age for summer-born children?

- How do you help settle an anxious starter?

- What do you do if a child is very upset at school?

- How do you deal with friendship issues and bullying?

- Do you have a peer-mentor or buddy scheme? (This is where older children are paired with new starters.)

- What sport and physical activity do children do?

- What are your school lunches like? Can I see a typical week's menu?

- How much time do children spend outside every day? How does this change as they get older?

- How much time do children spend sitting still and learning – for example, at a table, or at a computer?

- What is the school library like?

- What does an average school day look like?

- What opportunities are there for children who like art, music and drama?

- What is your SEND and pastoral-care provision like?

- What do you offer for 'gifted' children, or high achievers?

- What support do you provide for children who struggle academically?

- What is your view on standard assessments?

- What are the school values or ethos?

- What is the school's opinion of homework? When does it get set, how much and what sort of thing?

- What is your teacher retention rate like? How long have most of the current staff been here?

- Do you have an 'open-door policy' if parents have any concerns?

- Do you know how many siblings of current pupils will be applying this year?

- How many children are in an average class? How do you make sure they each get the individual attention they need?

- What clubs and extra-curricular activities do you run?

- What do you think parents would say about the school?

- What do you think pupils would say about the school?

- Do you think your current official rating is a good reflection of the school? If not, why?

- Does your school have an active PTA?

- What opportunities do you have for parents to get involved with the school?

- Do you offer school trips and visits? If so, what have they been in the past?

You shouldn't feel embarrassed about asking too many questions, but if you are conscious of time, or of monopolising a tour, ask the headteacher if you can send them some questions to answer via email, or speak to them on the phone at a later date. Usually, the response to this request is a pretty good indicator of the head's attitude, but do bear in mind that most are extremely stretched and while they may want to spare you the time to answer all of your questions as thoroughly as they can, it may just not be possible.

Warning signs to watch out for

School visits can be an opportunity to spot anything that might ring alarm bells. The following are things that you really don't want to see:

- **Quiet classrooms:** learning at infant and primary stages shouldn't be quiet. That doesn't mean it should be chaotic, but you should expect to hear talking and laughter. If a classroom is quiet, it may be an indication that the school expects too much compliance and age-inappropriate behaviour from the children; it can also be a sign that they aren't as engaged with their learning as they could be.

- **Sparse wall displays** A school should be proud to display its pupils' art- and project-work, even if it makes the walls look cluttered and non-colour-coordinated.

- **Unhappy children** Do the children look sad or stressed, or are they relaxed and smiling?

- **Stressed teachers** Do the teachers generally look happy at work? Or do they appear very tense? Or shouty?

- **No mess** Learning isn't neat and tidy. A classroom where everything is put away and looks pristine should raise suspicion, and while you don't want utter devastation either, somewhere in between shows a good balance.

- **Lack of outdoor play space or equipment** Outdoors is where children relax – you should be wary of a lack of space or equipment to facilitate this.

- **Children being disrespectful to each other** Are children polite to each other as well as to teachers? Do they hold doors open for each other, or help when another child drops something or falls over? A lack of compassion towards each other is often indicative of a lack of compassion and respect from teachers.

The secret to your child's happiness and success at school lies in choosing somewhere that is a good fit for their own unique needs, which can, and probably will, look different from those of your friend's child, so try hard to not be swayed by what other parents are doing and what a school looks like on paper.

Hopefully, this chapter has helped you to know what to look for and to consider when making your selection – but what happens once you've made that choice and know where your child will be going? Then it's all about the preparation, which is exactly what the next chapter will cover.

Chapter 4

Preparing Your Child to Start School

Once you've chosen and applied for your child's school place, there is a frustrating wait until you hear about their allocated space. The preparation you can put into starting school will be limited until you know exactly where you child will be going, but there are always things that you can do, both practically and emotionally in the interim. Then, once you know which school your child will be going to, you can increase the preparatory work. This chapter looks at what you can do, both immediately and over the coming months, to help your child to be ready for school and settle in well.

We will first consider the concept of 'school readiness' and what you need to teach your child before they start – as well as what you don't! We will then look at any purchases you need to make to ensure the easiest transition possible. Next, we'll deal with the more emotional preparation – how to help your child to look forward to school and reduce any anxiety. And finally, we'll think about preparing yourself – because in the business of preparing children, most parents forget that it is a huge transition for them too.

Educational school readiness

A question that seems to crop up again and again among discussion groups is, 'What do I need to teach my child so that they are ready for school?' This is commonly followed by questions such as, 'Do they need to know their ABCs?' 'Do I need to teach them to read?' 'Should we practise phonics?' 'Should they be able to write simple sentences?' I've even seen advertisements for 'pre-school coaching' – private tutoring sessions to get children up to speed with English and maths skills before they start school. And the good news is, your child doesn't need to be able to do any of these things. Preparation for schooling is much more about the everyday practicalities: skills that will enable your child to cope independently in the school environment and help them to feel happy and relaxed.

So what should you focus on teaching your child and doing with them over the coming months?

- **Read to them – lots** Get them to love books, by allowing them free choice and making story time a fun, interactive and enjoyable experience. Don't stress about teaching them letter recognition; just read, read and read to them some more.

- **Talk to them – lots** Encourage them to have conversations with you about things that interest them and how the world works. The thousand 'Why?' questions they seem to ask every day can be exceptionally annoying, but they are a great example of their natural curiosity, which, in turn, is a real learning attribute. If you don't know the answers to their questions, then say, 'I don't know, but let's figure it out together. Maybe we can find a film, book or website about it.' This natural learning that happens every day, purely organically, is much more powerful than trying to teach them formally.

- **Get out into nature with them** Enjoy these last few months of being able to spontaneously get outside for the day and plan trips away, whether it's enjoying time in your garden or that of a friend or family member, visiting local forests, woods, fields or nature reserves. Time spent outdoors is a great primer for school.

- **Prepare food with them** Cooking together can help to foster a love of good food, but it's also a great way to learn about maths and science skills organically: what temperature is the oven? Why do you add baking powder? What happens when you whisk or sift something? Encourage them to weigh items on your kitchen scales and so on. Cooking also helps to develop fine motor skills and tool control.

- **Messy play and painting** Messy play is important to encourage creativity and sensory experiences, while painting can help to express emotions, to learn about colours and shapes and, again, to encourage children to hold the paintbrush, pens and pencils correctly.

- **Work on their fine motor skills** This follows on from the previous point. Children don't need to start school knowing how to write, but they do need to know how to hold a pen and pencil. With less focus on arts and crafts and nature play these days, children frequently start school lacking in motor-control skills, and this can inhibit their ability to write.

- **Teach them to recognise their name when written**
  You needn't worry about teaching them to write their own name, but learning to recognise their name in writing is important, so that they can pick their name out of different labels – for instance, on their coat peg or drawer. If you do teach them to write their own name, however, make sure it is not all in capital letters, as this is a tricky habit for teachers to break. Instead, teach them to use a capital for the first letter and to do the rest in lower case.

Physical skills needed for school

There are quite a few specific physical skills that new school starters would ideally possess, each of which helps them with their independence and helps teachers and teaching assistants by reducing the amount of time they need to spend on tasks with children.

Here is a list of skills to work towards – it is a long one, so please don't be alarmed if your child can't do all these things by the time they start school; it's more of a guide than a 'tick-every-box' list:

- Teach them how to put on a cardigan/jumper (whichever their school uniform has) and coat – and take them off again.

- Teach them how to do a shirt up, or the few buttons on a polo shirt if they will not be wearing a traditional collared school shirt.

- Teach them how to put on gloves and return them to their coat pockets when they go in at the end of break time.

- Teach them how to sit on the floor with their legs crossed and hands in their laps.

- For children with long hair, teach them how to put a hair tie and/or clips in and take them out (so that they can do their own hair before and after PE lessons).

- Teach them how to undress, change into their PE kit and then put their uniform on again afterwards; as well as collect their kit and put it back into their PE bag.

- Teach them how to blow their nose and what to do with the tissue or handkerchief afterwards.

- Teach them how to hold a pencil.

- Teach them how to put up their hand if they want to ask a question.

- Tell them their teacher's name (when you know it) and the names of any teaching assistants (TAs).

- Teach them to go to the toilet independently, including wiping, flushing and washing hands afterwards.

- Tell them how to use a lock on a public-toilet door. It's especially helpful if you can find out what style of lock the school toilets have and find one like it to practise on.

- Teach them how to put on and take off shoes (on the correct feet – use the heart trick overleaf to help them identify left and right).

- Familiarise them with their own lunchbox and how to open and close it.

- Teach them to recognise their own belongings (e.g. their coat, bag, water bottle and so on – this includes recognising their name on any labels you use).

- Encourage them to drink water at home (as squash and milk won't be available during the day at school) and make sure they know how to open, close and refill their own water bottle.

- Teach them to peel satsumas and bananas if you will be putting them in their school lunch box.

- Make sure they can take the top off any yoghurt pots or pouches you will be giving them to take for school lunch.

- Teach them how to use a pair of scissors.

- Teach them how to spread glue with a spatula and use a glue stick.

- Teach them how to eat with a knife and fork and carry a tray with a plate of food on it.

THE HEART TRICK FOR PUTTING ON SHOES

Teaching children to put their shoes on the correct feet can be difficult and new school starters often come home with them the wrong way around. Using the heart trick below is a quick, simple and easy way of teaching them which shoe goes where. Use a permanent marker to draw half a heart on the inside of each shoe, so that when the shoes are placed together, the correct way, the two halves form a heart, like this:

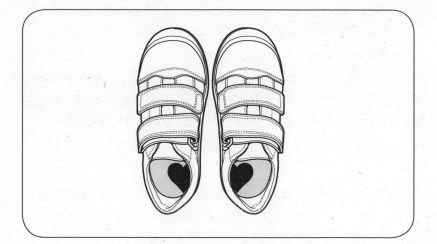

Practical preparations and purchases

A lot of the best preparations for starting school will be things you do and purchase yourself. Wise choices can make things a lot easier for your child. Here are some of my top tips:

- **Name absolutely everything** This includes lunchboxes, bottles, bags, all clothing, (even underwear and socks), shoes and PE kit.

- **Research the best name labels** The woven ones that you sew on are more time consuming, but far less likely to fall off – even the best sticky iron-on labels may not last a full school year, but some are much better than others. Ask friends and family for recommendations. Failing that, a permanent marker pen (to write on labels already in clothes) is an effective, long-lasting, cheap (and lazy) labelling tool.

- **Opt for Velcro school shoes** Laces or buckles can be incredibly fiddly and time-consuming to take off and put on.

- **For children who want to wear skirts** Opt for long, knee-length socks, rather than tights which can be complicated to put on and have a habit of falling down as the school day goes on; plus, they are not as durable as socks and tend to develop holes and ladders quickly.

- **Trousers and skirts** Go for elasticated waists that pull up and down easily.

- **Uniforms** Brand-name shoes and high-end uniforms aren't always the best; in fact, supermarket options tend not only to be good value, but last longer too. More expensive is not best when it comes to school uniform.

  Also, check with current and past parents at the school as to what uniform you really need to buy – for instance, how many logoed jumpers, sweatshirts and PE tops does/did their child use? These items can be very expensive, and you may not need everything that is recommended on the school list (or at least not in the quantities suggested).

  Lastly, keep an eye out for second-hand uniform sales. Lots of schools have a stall at their annual summer fete, while some have dedicated social-media groups or days when you can view items at the school. Keep a lookout on local selling sites too.

- **Lunch box** Choose one that is easy to open and close; if you have to grapple with it at all, then don't buy it.

- **Reusable bees-wax wraps** Try these instead of cling-film or aluminium foil – they are much better for the environment and usually easier for little hands to open.

- **Water bottle** Choose this with care. Make sure it really is leak-proof and that your child will be able to open and close it without difficulty (remember, they will need to refill it themselves during the day). Also, try to get one from a less common outlet (not a supermarket) or customise it, so that it is easier for your child to spot rather than being one of ten bottles that are all the same.

- **Long hair** Make sure this is tied back, preferably braided, to prevent the dreaded nits, which spread much quicker if hair is worn loose.

- **Pierced ears** Avoid doing this the summer before starting school, as they will still be healing at the beginning of term. Also, make sure you know the school policy on wearing earrings during PE lessons. Some schools expect children to take earrings out for lessons and put them back in after, which is usually well beyond the skill levels of most four- and five-year olds, and means earrings get lost and holes can close up very quickly.

- **Make the most of your time together** Go on special days out and consider creating a 'Before-I-start-school' bucket list.

- **Book a final term-time holiday** Take advantage of the lower prices – the difference between travel in term time and school holidays is phenomenal, the latter costing up to two or three times as much.

- **Social media** Join the social-media parents' group for new starters at your child's school if there is one; if there isn't, try setting one up. They can be lifesavers for last-minute 'What-do-they-need-to-bring-to-school today? questions and can also be a useful way to set up playdates over the summer, to introduce children to each other before school starts.

Again, don't be alarmed at the length of this list. Just take on board the points that resonate with you.

Packed lunches and school dinners

If your child's school offers the option of school dinners, it is a good idea to prepare for them before the beginning of term. Most schools will be able to provide sample menus to give you an idea of the sort of food that is offered. If the foods are new to your child, it can be helpful to introduce them in the safety of their home environment in advance, so that they may be more likely to try the food at school and, importantly, will recognise what something is by name. School dinners are usually served on plastic divider plates, so again, if you can find out which plates and cutlery are used, you can familiarise your child with them at home, so that they are used to them by the time they start school. Finally, if your child drinks anything other than water with meals, slowly encourage them to drink water, as this is likely to be the only drink on offer at school.

If your child has any special dietary requirements, ask the school for the contact details of the catering company, so that you can speak to them in advance to talk through what is on offer and how they can meet your child's needs. Some schools and catering companies are better at this than others. My son has coeliac disease (an autoimmune condition, as a result of which he cannot eat gluten). The school were able to provide food for him, but rather than offer gluten-free alternatives, they gave him whatever food they had that was naturally gluten-free. This meant lots of baked potatoes, salad and plain meat and vegetables, followed by jelly or fruit for dessert. This sounds fine, until you understand that his friends were eating pasta, bread, pies, cakes, cookies and the like right next to him, meaning that he felt very excluded. Sadly, we had to stop school dinners pretty quickly, as we found it much easier to help him feel included by providing our own food. Other schools, however, are brilliant at catering to special dietary requirements. Just make sure in advance that when your school says they can cater for your child you know exactly what that means.

When it comes to packed lunches, most schools usually have rules in place as to what you may and may not take in. If there is a child at the school who has a nut allergy, for example, then nuts in all forms will be banned from packed lunches (including things like nut butters, cereal bars and energy balls containing nuts and anything baked with almond flour). Schools also commonly ban cakes and/or chocolate bars, as well as fizzy drinks from lunches. If your child takes in contraband and they are caught with it, then the forbidden items are likely to be confiscated. Do make sure, therefore, that you are aware of any lunch-box rules in advance.

Managing medical issues

If your child has an allergy or illness, you will need to notify the school, usually when completing the initial paperwork. Sometimes schools request copies of doctors' letters to keep on file; this is especially true if your child needs medication administered during the school day. If your child's allergy or illness is more severe, or unusual, then it would be a good idea to contact the school in advance of them starting (before the end of the previous school year) to request a meeting with whoever will be their teacher, their teaching assistant and the school nurse, if there is one. Take with you any literature that you have explaining the allergy or illness, and check that everybody who needs to understands how it may affect your child and what is required of them. Also, discuss who will administer any medication and how and where it will be stored. Finally, make sure that the school has any emergency contact details (someone other than you who knows about and understands your child's condition) in case there is a problem and they cannot get in touch with you.

Childcare preparations

For those who work, starting school usually means new childcare arrangements. Here are some things to consider:

- **Wraparound childcare** (i.e. before and after school; see also page 65). Does the school have onsite facilities for this? Or is there one locally that transports children to and from school? If you have no club-based childcare available, are there local childminders who offer a similar service? Make sure that you find out how early you need to put your child's name down to guarantee a place with any of these, and ask if you can visit a few times before your child starts to help them to settle in.

- **School runs** Who will be taking your child to and from school? If you will be doing the school run yourself, but timing is tight for you to get to and from work in time, make sure that you do some practice runs to check on traffic levels. If others will be sharing the school run with you, set a rota up well in advance, so that everybody is sure of what they are doing and when.

- **School holidays** Many clubs that offer wraparound care also offer special school-holiday clubs, and there are often sports-based clubs operating out of local leisure complexes offering holiday care too. There may also be other parents in the same situation as you who you can set up a childcare circle with, each of you taking off one or two days per week to look after each other's children, so that none of you needs to pay for childcare. Planning in advance and saving up any paid leave at the start of the year and booking it for school holidays is another idea. You will be able to find the term dates for your county at least a year in advance on your local authority's website.

- **When your child is sick** When illness inevitably strikes, what will your childcare plan be? Do you have friends or relatives near by who can help? Or will you need to take time off work at short notice? Make sure you know your rights both legally and contractually at your place of work.

Of course, one of the biggest positives of children starting school is usually a reduction in childcare fees, so although there may be some tricky new scenarios to navigate, there is a positive side too.

Preparing your child emotionally

It's never too early to begin preparing your child emotionally for starting school. You can start talking about the school day and what children do at school, even before you know which one your child will be going to. The more you normalise school – for instance, pointing them out when you drive or walk past, looking at uniform in shops and noting what children are wearing, watching television programmes that feature schools and reading books about them – the more you will take some of the unknown, and thus the fear, out of the transition.

Nevertheless, any preparation you might do can be a lot less effective than you'd imagine and hope for. This is because young children possess minimal hypothetical thought and abstract-thinking processing skills. This means that they can't predict the future (not in a mystical sense) and how it will affect them. And they also struggle with things that aren't tangible. For instance, they may understand the concept of school, but will not be able to imagine themselves there. Hypothetical and abstract-thinking skills do not mature until the end of primary schooling, so, until that point it's fair to say that the results of any emotional preparation work you do will be limited. That's not to say it's not worth doing, as some of it will have an effect – just don't base all your hopes on it. This is why I focus so much more on practical preparation – because the more you ensure things run smoothly on a practical level (the elements you really can control), the easier children will find things emotionally.

What if your child does not want to go?

While some children are positively chomping at the bit to get to school, for many there is great trepidation. Children can be incredibly fearful about beginning school and can be adamant that they do not want to go. Be careful not to take this at face value because what most are saying is simply that there is an element of starting school that worries them. This might be:

- not wanting to be away from you

- not wanting to leave younger siblings (especially alone with you)

- concern about missing their normal everyday routines and activities

- not wanting to leave their current nursery, childminder or preschool

- feeling scared of the unknown

- feeling nervous about meeting new children and adults

- feeling unsure about what to expect of school

- feeling uncomfortable in their new uniform.

While these are all undoubtedly valid reasons for children to be anxious and upset about, none of them is insurmountable, nor is it the case that school is the wrong place for them or that they will have a horrible time when they are there.

One of the most common themes arising from conversations with teachers when I was researching this book was that of children telling their parents they didn't want to go to school when they were being dropped off. The teachers all told me, independently, that they wished the parents could see how their children were during the school day – that even those who were the most adamant that they didn't want to be there had fun and were happy and settled. It's only natural for children to be nervous about starting school, just as we are when we take on something new. Imagine starting a new job, for example; you would feel many of the things in the list above, the difference being that your thinking and vocabulary are mature enough to allow you to articulate why you are worried about starting and how you are feeling. But whereas you can verbalise and rationalise the specific elements of the new job that worry you, children tend to just say, 'I don't want to go' – and leave it at that.

What can you do to help them? Again, the key here is as

much preparation as you can do, trying to take away the unknown, as far as possible. This includes: practice school runs; wearing their uniform at home in the run-up to school starting, so it doesn't feel too new; wearing new school shoes around the house to break them in; meeting children who will be in their class, preferably for playdates, as well as at official settling-in sessions; meeting teachers; familiarising them with the school. Reassure them that you will still have weekends to spend together, and tell them that you will miss them too, but that you will always be there at the end of the day and they never have to wait too long to see you again. Focus on the fun stuff that they will do at school, speaking about all the activities and equipment you know they will enjoy and downplaying what you will be doing during the day (to reduce any fear of missing out).

When they tell you that they don't want to go, try to find out a little more detail about what they are feeling. Empathise with them, saying, for example, 'You are going to miss me; I know that makes you feel sad,' while hugging them. But then build their confidence: 'But I know that you will make new friends and have fun at school too'. Validate their emotions, but don't enable them to become something bigger than they already are. You need to help them to focus on the positive and examine their feelings for what they are – anxieties about certain aspects of school, not the whole of it. Do make sure that their teacher is aware of their worries. They will be very experienced at helping anxious children to settle; they may even have special programmes or activities in place or may offer some extra settling-in sessions. One thing is for sure: your child won't be the first at the school to feel like this. Many children who are now settled and happy at school start off from a place of anxiety initially.

Settling-in sessions

Schools will usually offer one or two settling-in sessions before your child starts school. These are very important, so do everything you can to attend. Some will run sessions for parents/carers and children together in an informal play-based setting, others will run more formal 'taught' sessions for just the children and some favour an approach incorporating both.

If your child is feeling particularly anxious and doesn't want to separate from you, ask the school if you can remain in the classroom for some or all of the session, and find out in advance what will happen, so that you can discuss it with your child to prepare them. After the session, check with the teacher what took place, so that you can talk to your child about it at home (they're not always the most reliable at telling you what they did at school at this age). Again, focus on the fun aspects and things that can help to build some excitement for your child to start properly.

Helping your child to know what to expect

The more children understand and can predict what will happen during the school day, the less likely they are to be anxious about it. School is a big step for them and much of the day is taken up with activities that are entirely new to them. Talking through different parts of the day, using visual props – such as photographs, books and videos – or role play can help children to feel less worried about their start. Here are some things to think about:

- **Familiarise them with the basic structure of the day**
  Start with going into the classroom, hanging up coats

and settling down on the carpet/rug or chairs, then playtimes, lunch, different activities and getting ready to come home. Creating a visual timetable or a scrapbook is a lovely idea; simply find pictures of children at school doing different things (such as eating lunch or doing PE) and either stick them in the scrapbook in chronological order or place them on a wall or large sheet of paper, with Blu Tack or sticky fixers, starting with the beginning of the school day at the top and finishing with the end of the day at the bottom.

- **Make sure they know where to put their things** For instance, where should they hang their coat? Where do their book bags go? Where is their PE kit stored? Where do they put their lunch boxes and water bottles? These are things to ask their teacher and request that they are covered at any settling-in sessions.

- **Talk to them about what happens during break times** How often do they get a playtime? Where do they go to play? What can they play with? If they are having school dinners you can role-play queuing up to be served, holding their plate and pointing to whichever food choice they want.

- **Run through a few of the typical school activities with them** Try having a pretend PE lesson (where they put on their PE kit and change into their uniform afterwards) and a story time, sitting on the carpet. You can even take a pretend register in the morning, where your child practises saying, 'Yes Mr/Mrs/Miss xxxx' when their name is called out (this works even better if you know the names of the other children, so you can call them out too).

Separation anxiety

Perhaps the most common reason children give for not wanting to go to school is that they do not want to be separated from you. Some are genuinely too young, or otherwise not ready, for the separation. For them, either delaying a year, introducing a part-time start, or even considering home-education is the best solution. Most will adapt to the transition quickly though, usually over a period of a couple of weeks. There are a few effective and gentle ways to help them to cope with the separation:

- Draw a heart on your hand, on your palm, and draw another on their palm, in the same position as the one on yours. Hold your hands up to each other, palm to palm and tell your child that you will always be connected – that there will always be a little bit of you in them and vice versa and that the heart is a reminder of this. Tell them that when they are missing you, they should touch the heart on their hand and remember that you and they are connected and will always come back together again.

- Find some embroidery thread (something stronger than regular cotton), in a colour your child loves. Unravel the thread and tie one end around their wrist, like a bracelet, then tie the other end around your wrist, in the same way. There will be a long piece of thread between you. Don't cut it just yet. Tell your child, 'These bracelets connect us, just like they do right now, with this thread joining me to you.' Then, cut the thread and say, 'We may not be joined by the thread any more, but these bracelets are always a reminder of our connection and how we are always joined, even if we are not together.' Encourage them to touch the bracelet and think about that joining thread when you are apart, and they are feeling sad.

- Make some 'bravery spray'. Use a travel-size spray bottle and fill it with water and a drop of food colouring in their favourite colour, adding some edible glitter too for extra magic. Blow some kisses into the mixture before replacing the top. Then explain that if they are feeling scared when they are away from you, all they need to do is to spray it once or twice into their mouth, or on to their body somewhere and the power of your kisses will help them to feel braver.

If you use one of these techniques, do make sure you make the teacher aware, so that they don't confiscate the bravery spray, wipe off the heart mark or tell the child to take their bracelet off.

Preparing yourself to be separated from your child

So far, the focus has been on preparing children for starting school. But in my experience of working with thousands of parents in your position, the parents – particularly mothers – need as much preparation emotionally as their children, if not more. Your 'baby' starting school is a tremendous transition for you. It feels oddly bittersweet. You're very proud of them, looking so grown up, and yet you yearn for the baby they once were. They can also look incredibly tiny, next to the older children at the school who tower over them like giants. Understandably, this can trigger a protection mechanism in you, as a parent, to run in and protect them. Added to this is the anxiety about how they will be. Will they be upset? Will somebody comfort them if they cry? (The answer is yes, by the way.) Will they make friends? Will they be OK without you? Will they cope with everything they have to learn?

The trouble is, anxiety is catching. Children look to their parents/caregivers to know how to behave. If they see that you are worried that they won't cope well at school, it can subconsciously erode their confidence. Your anxiety can add to theirs and you will soon find yourself in a perpetual cycle of shared worry. As the adult, it is so important that you break this cycle, or preferably prevent it from happening at all.

Acknowledge your feelings and try to work with them in a mindful and positive way, so that you can fill your child with a sense of pride, confidence and happy anticipation, rather than doubt and fear. There is no one way to do this; different methods work for different people. Here are a couple of ideas:

- Try recognising what you're feeling and rationalising that it's OK to feel it, but resolve that you are not going to let it overcome you, breathing deeply, grounding yourself and remembering all the work you have put in and the resilience your child shows.

- Imagine an anxiety dial in your head, turning it down from 'highly anxious' on the right, to 'completely calm' on the left. Picture the needle moving to the left as you breathe and allow some of the anxiety to leave you. You probably won't get to 'completely calm', but 'less anxious' is a good start.

Sometimes when our children start school it can drag up painful memories for us. If you were bullied at school, found it hard to make friends, had a teacher who made you feel insecure or you felt uncomfortable for any reason, recognise that these are *your* feelings. They are not the feelings of your child and their experience is a new and unique one, not yours repeated. Your child's time at school could be entirely different from anything you went through, or anything you fear now. If these feelings are very strong, then do consider talking to a mental-health professional about them. You don't have to feel like this. Seeking help can bring about positive change for you, leaving you feeling happier and more settled – and, importantly, you don't need to continue the cycle with your child. Ultimately, a calm and self-assured parent is far more likely to have a child who takes the transition to school in their stride, borrowing some of the confidence of their parent.

The next chapter will look a little more at your feelings, including what to do if you think you're going to cry at the school drop-off and how to fill your time and any empty space you are left with, whether that is actual free time/space if you stay home, or metaphorical, if you work. It will also deal with the immediate run-up to school starting – days, rather than weeks or months before – and the first day itself, as well as how you can help your child to settle in once they have started.

Chapter 5

The First Day and Settling In

N ow the big day is nearly here, what do you do? The last few days at home may be a strange dichotomy of dragging on for ever and whizzing by before you can stop and take a breath. There are many things to consider at this stage, including the first few drop-offs and pick-ups, what to expect of your child when they come home from school and how to get them to open up to you about what they did, as well as your own feelings and how they can impact your child, which we will revisit here.

The last few days before school

This period can pass in a blur of uniform-buying, labelling, haircuts and packing everything into bags. Ideally, what children really need to do with this time is to spend it with you, relaxing and having fun. Try to get the practical preparation out of the way with at least a week or two to spare and use this time to really focus on your connection with your child, keeping them calm and making the most of the free time you have left together. If you work and have any holiday to spare, it's a lovely idea to book a long weekend off (this may or may not coincide with the August bank holiday, depending on where in the world you live and when the school year starts).

Get outside in nature as much as possible – going for walks or to the park – or spend time at home doing crafts, playing games or baking together. Your goal here should be screen-free activities that stimulate conversation. Avoid focusing all the conversation on starting school though; instead, use the time to check in on how your child is feeling and discuss any worries or concerns they may have in general. By getting the practical preparation out of the way first and spending a week or two relaxing and bonding, you will avoid that last-minute panic that can cause children to feel unsettled and nervous. This will make for a much easier school start.

The importance of trial runs

Before your child starts school, make sure you know how long the journey will take; whether you are planning to walk, cycle or drive, time it at the same time of day, but be aware that there will be more traffic on the roads once school starts and add on time accordingly. You could also time how long it takes for your child to get up, washed, brush their teeth and hair, have their breakfast and get dressed (including putting shoes on). A lot of school-run stress is due to us, as parents, not allowing enough time for the child to get ready. A few practice runs will give you a realistic idea of how long things will take and what time you must get up on a school day. My answer to parents who ask me, 'How do I get my child out of the house on time?' is: 'Get up earlier!' It's the one thing you have absolute control over, and it's much easier to change ourselves than to try to change our children. Practice runs also take some of the unfamiliarity out of starting school, so it is less of a big deal once starting day arrives.

A good bedtime routine

Sleep is something that's often overlooked when it comes to school readiness, but an overtired child is not one who will settle in well. The weeks and months in the run-up to school starting are an important time to sort your child's sleep, so that it is as healthy and restful as possible.

HOW MUCH SLEEP DO CHILDREN NEED?

The National Sleep Foundation recommends that children aged four and five, get between ten and thirteen hours of sleep in a twenty-four-hour period.[1] For those aged six through to thirteen, the recommendation is between nine and eleven hours. These ranges are obviously quite broad, but with good reason. Sleep needs are individual. Some children will naturally need less than others and will thrive on nine or ten hours a night, whereas others innately need a lot more and will struggle with fewer than twelve.

The key is in understanding your child's own unique needs. Not pushing them to take too much sleep if they naturally need less is just as important as not being sleep-deprived if they need more. My recommendation for a specific bedtime for school-aged children is somewhere around

7.30–8 p.m. By this, I mean the actual sleep-onset time, not the time you start their bedtime or tuck them up in bed with stories. Research from the USA has shown that young children have a surge of melatonin (the sleep hormone) at around 7.30 p.m., therefore trying to put them to bed before this may make bedtime much longer and harder, because they are not chemically ready to sleep.[2] Finding the sweet spot of a biologically appropriate bedtime really helps in the evenings. Of course, if your child has to be asleep by 7 p.m. because they need more sleep, then that's OK, so long as you – and they – are happy with their earlier bedtime.

Bedtime routines

Children are regularly separated from their parents during the day in term time. This separation and the subsequent need to reconnect in the evenings can, and often does, play havoc with bedtime.

The answer to any trouble that arises from this separation (whether in the form of not going to sleep, more waking in the night or difficult behaviour in the evenings) is to schedule in reconnection playtime every evening, between dinner and bedtime. I know many parents will read that and think: But I don't have time for that; it's too late; I'm tired; I need adult time. However, a delayed bedtime facilitates that all-important regrouping, which means an easier, quicker bedtime and less night waking – a trade-off you might, ultimately, consider worthwhile.

Ideally, your reconnection time would last for between thirty minutes and an hour. It should be spent fully engaged in playing with your child. For the majority (at least three quarters) of the time, make play as loud, crazy and busy as possible. Try to incorporate lots of running around, roughhousing and being really silly. In the warmer weather, it's great to spend time outside, in the garden or park. Think of it as having a puppy who needs to burn off their excess energy, ready to be crated for the night. A young child is no different, except that for them play spells connection too. It's important that your child leads the play as much as possible and that screens don't feature at all (so no TV, tablets or smartphones). Towards the end of the reconnection period, go into your main living area and focus on quiet time, such as reading books, drawing, doing puzzles and so on (once again though, no screens). This is preparing the child for bedtime, so keep it as calm, quiet and still as possible.

Once the quiet play has ended, it signals that bedtime is shortly about to begin, but just before this, I recommend giving your child a quick bedtime snack. My snack of choice is wholewheat toast with almond butter or porridge/oatmeal with sliced bananas (these snacks contain good levels of tryptophan and magnesium – nutrients that are needed for good sleep). When snack time is over, it's time for bedtime to begin. My only proviso with this is that you don't go back to the main living area again – you only go to the bathroom and the room your child sleeps in. Nowhere else.

A TYPICAL EVENING WITH A NEW SCHOOL STARTER

Here is a quick run down of what a typical evening might look like for your new school starter. I've based this on a bedtime (sleep onset) of 8 p.m., but you can juggle times to suit you and your child, especially if you work. This is just to give you an idea; it's not a hard-and-fast prescription.

- 5–5.30 p.m.: free playtime, while dinner is prepared
- 5.30–6 p.m.: dinner time
- 6–6.45 p.m.: crazy and loud active play (no screens)
- 6.45–7 p.m.: calmer, quiet play (no screens)
- 7–7.15 p.m.: bedtime snack
- 7.15 p.m.: prepare the bedroom for sleep
- 7.20–7.30 p.m.: bathtime and brush teeth
- 7.40–7.45 p.m.: change into pyjamas
- 7.45 p.m.: into bed for story time and lots of cuddles
- 8:00 p.m.: sleep onset

Do try to keep to the same timings at weekends – lie-ins and late nights are disorientating for the developing circadian rhythm and can be quite damaging to a child's sleep. Consistency, especially during school holidays, is ultimately much better for children.

The combination of reconnection time, a physiologically appropriate bedtime, snack before bed and consistent routine can really help your child to sleep well and reduce any stress at bedtime, making it much easier for them to cope well at school.

Common sleep problems in school-aged children

Sadly, sleep problems are fairly common throughout childhood. Modern-day society seems to believe that once a baby turns six or twelve months, the broken nights and tricky bedtimes are behind you. This is frustratingly not true. But the good news is that as children get older, night waking lessens dramatically, aside from the odd nightmare or bedwetting. Most sleep problems in older childhood usually centre on bedtime resistance and early-morning waking.

Here is a breakdown of the main sleep problems for school-aged children – and how to fix them:

1. **Incorrect expectations** These top the list as the cause of most sleep problems in childhood. Parents are commonly worried that their children are not getting enough sleep, so try to encourage an earlier bedtime, but, in many cases, this is at odds with what the child needs biologically. As stated earlier, if your child naturally needs less sleep, trying to force them to do otherwise is going to end in disaster. They will resist going to sleep, which makes them secrete cortisol (the stress hormone), which, in turn, inhibits melatonin and will mean they end up going to sleep even later. The best thing parents can do is try to understand the true biological sleep needs at each age and make sure they are not trying to get their child to sleep for too long.

2. **Timing** As with expectations, above, the actual time of sleep matters too. We have unusually early bedtimes in the UK, USA, Canada and Australia. In most parts of Asia, children don't go to bed until 10 p.m. and research shows that Asian parents have far fewer problems than UK parents with sleep.[3] Expecting children to sleep before their melatonin rise can cause problems (see page 108) and this is even worse in the spring and summer, when it's still light outside when we try to make children go to sleep, because light exposure has a huge effect on melatonin release. A later bedtime also allows for that all-important reconnection time (see page 108).

3. **Nightmares, fears and anxieties** Nightmares are extremely common in young children and can intensify

when they start school, as their imaginations are filled with images from stories, television programmes, historic events and shared myths and legends. Reducing scary stimuli and carefully vetting what children are exposed to at home, both in books and what they watch, can be helpful. Speaking to them about their fears and anxieties can help too, especially if they have learned something that upset them at school. You can also use tools to counter their fears. These include worry dolls/eaters (stuffed animals with a zip-mouth opening into which you place a piece of paper where you've written their fears for the friendly monsters to eat), dream catchers and monster spray (the same as the bravery spray, mentioned in Chapter 4 – but using a different colour glitter or food colouring and sprayed around the bedroom; a drop of lavender here is helpful too as it helps to induce calm).

If your child wakes in the night from a nightmare, don't be afraid to let them come into your bed if it soothes them. Meeting their needs and comforting them is not a bad habit; far from it – your nurturing actions now will aid the development of the emotion-regulation part of their brains, which means that they will able to calm and settle themselves independently more quickly than if they were left to deal with their fears and anxiety alone.

4. **Poor bedtime routines** We all need bedtime routines, whatever our age. However, they tend to go out of the window a little bit once the toddler years are over. Children need time to wind down and to have clear markers and boundaries at bedtime. A great routine would involve a bath, reading a book together, tucking up in bed and having an end-of-day chat, followed by an audiobook or a special kids' relaxation recording.

Keeping the evening and bedtime routine the same every day is key for good sleep. Families are often so busy nowadays that bedtime routines are overlooked, especially when children start school, but they're really important. In fact, according to research, they are the most important predictor of child sleep.[4]

5. **Diet** Most young children don't consume enough iron- or magnesium-rich foods, and research has shown that deficiencies in both cause sleep problems.[5] Similarly, omega-3 deficiency has been linked to less sleep in children, with difficulties falling asleep and sleep disorders such as night terrors being more common in children who are deficient.[6] Having said that, there are also a lot of myths surrounding diet and sleep, perhaps the most common being that sugary foods inhibit sleep – they don't.[7] Many parents avoid sugar for their children in the belief that it causes hyperactivity and sleep problems, when the real culprits are usually the artificial additives that many sugary foods contain.[8]

6. **Screen exposure and lighting** Research has shown that being exposed to screens two hours before bed has a very negative impact on sleep for children, even if it's a special bedtime-themed children's programme.[9] The programmes overstimulate the brain and the screens release blue light, causing the brain to inhibit the release of melatonin. Turning off TVs, tablets and smartphones at least two hours before your child's sleep-onset time (including those that you are using yourself) is vital and children should never have screens of any sort in their bedrooms.

   Similarly, lighting at bedtime is important too. You should never use the main overhead light, or even a lamp with a regular bulb in their rooms at bedtime, as these also secrete blue light (especially if you use energy-saving bulbs which give off a very blue wavelength). Nightlights are usually bad news too. If your child has a nightlight that is white, blue, pink, green purple or even some shades of yellow (in terms of the light colour emitted), then it's best to remove it from their bedroom. These light sources all inhibit melatonin release and are like putting a giant sun in their bedroom. Instead, look for a low-blue-light lamp or red nightlight.

7. **Enlarged adenoids/sleep apnoea** If your child snores, is a heavy mouth-breather, or is prone to ear infections or frequent colds, they may have enlarged adenoids. Adenoids are composed of lymphatic tissue and form part of the immune system which helps to fight infection; they are located behind the nose and top of the mouth. If they become swollen, they can obstruct breathing, particularly at night. Enlarged adenoids can cause disrupted sleep, loud snoring and, in a few extreme cases, obstructive sleep apnoea, where the adenoids are so enlarged that they prevent breathing through the nose. This can result in lowered oxygen saturations and highly disrupted sleep patterns, which can cause exhaustion during the daytime. If you suspect this may be affecting your child, then you should arrange a visit to your family doctor.

8. **Bedwetting** Wetting the bed, or enuresis, to give it its proper medical name, is common in younger school-aged children. According to research, 8 per cent of four-and-a-half-year-olds wet the bed at least twice every week and 21 per cent show infrequent (less than twice per week) wetting.[10]

Bedwetting can often increase when children start school, especially if they find the experience stressful.

Despite the obvious disruption to sleep that comes with bedwetting, it is not considered a medical problem until the child reaches seven years of age. Until this point, perhaps the easiest way to cope with it is to be prepared, making the bed with several layers of sheets and water-proof mats, so that when the child wets you can simply take off the top wet layer, leaving a dry and fresh one underneath, without having to strip the whole bed.

Never punish or shout at a child who has wet the bed; they have no control over their accidents and chastising them often makes things worse. Similarly, don't reward them for dry nights – again, it is not something they have conscious control over and on nights when they do wet, the lack of reward can leave them feeling incredibly upset and dent their self-esteem. Instead, try your hard-est to take a deep breath, bite your tongue and help them to understand that it's OK – it's common and normal and you're not angry with them.

Sleep is not a static process. By this I mean it has many ups and downs, which are often related to how your child is feel-ing emotionally. Just like adults, children can have problems getting to sleep if they are feeling anxious or overwhelmed. For this reason, the ultimate answer to most sleep issues in school-aged children is simply time, patience, reassurance and a tonne of love until they pass.

The day and night before the first day of school

So the big day is almost here. What should you plan for the day and night before?

- Take the day off if you can, so that you can be together with your child and supportive of any worries and meltdowns.

- Don't plan any big events that might overstimulate your child the day before school, and potentially make them struggle with sleep that evening.

- Encourage your child to get out their uniform and lay it out ready for the morning (including their underwear, socks and shoes).

- Pack their PE kit together with them; but do check if they need to take it in on Day 1 – most schools don't.

- Ask your child to get their water bottle and school bag prepared, placing them somewhere near your front door, ready to pick up in the morning.

- Explain, or role play what you will do in the morning when they wake up.

- Check in with how they're feeling. This is the time for any last-minute chats about nerves and fears.

- Plan a relaxing evening, limit screen time, have a good connecting playtime and give them a warm lavender-scented bath (or shower if they prefer).

- Don't make bedtime too early. Many parents make the mistake of saying 'Early bedtime tonight because you have a big day tomorrow and need to rest' – but this is usually counterproductive, causing worry over getting to sleep if they are not biologically ready (see page 108). These early nights usually result in a sleep onset far later than if you had not tried to bring bedtime forward.

- Make sure you have any medication the school may need during the day, packed and labelled with your child's name (with instructions, if necessary).

- Pre-prepare and pack any lunch the night before to save time in the morning.

When all is done and your child is tucked up in bed, it's time to focus on you. Tomorrow is a big day, not only for your child, but for you too. For the easiest, calmest morning and drop-off, you need to be feeling relaxed and calm yourself. The rest of the evening is yours to do whatever relaxes you the most and fuels you with an air of confidence and composure the next day – because however you are feeling, your child will pick up on it and will be likely to copy.

The big day

Perhaps the best tip I can give you for the very first day of school is to set your alarm early and take some time, before your child wakes, to check in with your own feelings. Have a calm breakfast and a hot drink, take a short walk outside, take a long, leisurely shower and breathe deeply. The best gift you can give your child on their first day is a calm parent. If you have prepared well the day before, you will have little to do practically speaking, so you should be able to devote the time to getting into the right headspace to support your child.

The first drop-off

You've reached the final hurdle – saying goodbye at the first school drop-off – and there are a few questions about this that crop up time and again:

- **Should you drop them off in the playground or go into the classroom with them?** This depends very much on the individual school and teacher. Some will be happy for parents to enter the classroom, whereas others prefer children to go in independently right from the start. Parents can be worried about this, as they want to go in and help their children to hang up their belongings, find somewhere to sit and to feel settled, but the consensus among teachers is that this tends to unsettle them much more than saying goodbye in the playground. If they are encouraged to be independent from the very beginning, they usually embrace the whole experience more quickly.

- **What do you do if your child is reluctant to leave you?** Despite the best preparation and plans, children can become very reluctant to leave your side. Remember, they aren't saying they don't want to go to school at all; rather, this is about them being worried about leaving you or missing you. The first place to start here is feeling confident in your school choice and preparation and helping your child to see some of that confidence. Don't belittle them; hear and recognise their feelings – 'You're sad that we won't see each other and you will miss me', or, 'You're scared because this is all new' – but try to reassure them ('I will miss you too, but we will see each other again very soon; remember I always come back', or, 'It's OK to be scared; the other children are too, but soon you will feel happy and I bet you will enjoy your day and make new friends'). Remind your child of their comfort cues (the heart on their hand that matches yours, the bravery spray or the thread around your wrists that always joins you – see page 101).

- **What should you do if they cry?** The answer here is almost identical to the previous one. Let them know it's OK to cry; don't be tempted to say, 'Don't be silly, don't cry', or, 'You're OK, stop crying', as this unconsciously diminishes their feelings and sends them a message that you don't really care how they feel. If they get very upset, walk with them to see their teacher, teaching assistant or another member of staff and ask if they can help – this may be your first time taking a crying child to school, but they will have experienced it many times before and will have lots of tips and tricks up their sleeve. Also, don't presume that your child's whole day will be sad because they were crying when they went into the classroom; often, a child will completely change and be having great fun only five or ten minutes after sobbing in their parent's arms.

- **What if *you* cry?** This is one of the reasons why I suggested waking early on the first day (see page 117), as it makes extra time for all your emotions and gives you a chance to get a lot of the tears out before you set foot on the school playground. Most parents will cry on their child's first day of school. Some will have full-on sobbing sessions, whereas others will discreetly wipe a tear from their eye. If you look around the playground, you won't be the only one fighting back the tears. Allow your emotions, all of them. Just make sure your child knows that you're not crying because of them, or because anything bad will happen; instead, while they are still with you, try to focus on the excitement and fun they will have at school, then let it all out when you leave.

- **What if you're working, or can't drop them off for other reasons?** Not every parent gets to take their child to school on their first day. For whatever reason, sometimes this is just not possible. I would say that children tend to do better if they are not dropped off by the parent they have the strongest bond with. There are usually far fewer tears and clinging. So it isn't always a bad thing if you're not there, and it could make for a much smoother start for your child. Just make sure that whoever is taking your child takes lots of photos and video (school rules permitting) for you to watch later.

The end of the school day

This is something that can bring about entirely different concerns and worries. You will be eager to hear what your child has been up to all day, whereas for them, telling you what they did probably won't be high up on their list of things to discuss with you. The end of the school day can often bring about unexpected tricky behaviour too.

Picking them up

You may have spent all day wondering what your child is doing and how they are, while they have probably been having fun and expending lots of energy. It's safe to expect that they will be hungry and thirsty, so you should plan ahead and take a drink and a snack with you to school, so you can offer this to your child before you even begin to ask how their day went.

Finding out about their day

Can you remember a time at the end of a school day when a parent asked you, 'So what did you do today?' I can, vividly. It used to annoy me, and I remember grunting a quick 'OK' in response. My parents would always try to tease more from me, and I was hardly ever forthcoming. Why did it annoy me? Mostly because I was tired after a busy day, or because sometimes I didn't feel great – either emotionally or physically. I just wanted to relax, after a day of stimulation, talking and trying to be on my best behaviour. Of course, I loved my parents – they were my safe place at the end of a day apart. And I knew I didn't have to talk to them or pretend any more, so I would ignore them or refuse to be drawn into conversation. Sometimes I simply couldn't remember what I'd done all day

When we bombard children with questions about their day the minute we see them, we are no longer their safe place to relax. But does this mean you shouldn't speak to children about their day? No, it doesn't. However, there are ways to do so that acknowledge the child's feelings and encourage them to communicate with you when they are ready. The following tips can really help your child to feel safe, relaxed and more likely to tell you about their day:

- **Give them time** Don't ask questions as soon as you pick them up. Make it a priority to create a calming, soothing and supportive space in your presence for at least the first half hour, if not an hour. Don't be alarmed by any rudeness or unpleasant behaviour in this time either; think of it as your child discharging all the stress of the day.

- **Make sure they have had a drink and snack first** Very young children are used to being able to eat and drink whenever they are hungry and thirsty at home, but when they start school, they must eat to a prescribed schedule. This often means they need a snack as soon as they get home – if not before, on the journey home.

- **Give them a chance to unwind in their own way** This might be playing with a favourite toy, reading stories with them, cuddling up on the sofa, or watching television (screen time isn't all bad – just avoid it before bedtime).

- **Get involved in their play if they invite you** Play is by far the best way to reconnect at the end of a day apart. Try to put your phone away for half an hour (or more if you can), get down on the floor and play with your child. If they don't invite you to join them, ask, 'Can I play with you?' – try to let them lead the play as much as possible and don't be afraid to be silly.

Only at this point is it time to ask about their day (if they haven't told you already), being mindful about how you ask them. 'What did you do today?' is a big question. It asks a lot of them – sometimes too much – and the overwhelming question will often meet with dismissive answers. It's far better to ask short and specific questions. Here are some examples:

- What was the best thing that happened today?

- What did you not enjoy today?

- What made you laugh today?

- Did you feel proud of anything you did today?

- What did you learn today that you thought was interesting?

- Did you do anything today that you thought was really boring?

- What was your favourite part of your lunchtime break?

- What did you play at break time?

Sometimes, the funnier and quirkier the questions, the better. Here are some fun questions (they might seem a little strange at first, but they can often provide a good insight into how the child is feeling and coping socially):

- If your teacher was an animal, which one would s/he be?

- Which child in your class do you think would be the best superhero?

- Who in the school would you most like to be abducted by aliens?

- Who would make the best mean and grumpy witch at your school?

- Who would make the best, kindest, nicest fairy at your school?

- If you could make up a special song for people to sing at school, what would it be?

As a rule, aim to ask no more than a couple of questions per day, unless your child seems to be enjoying answering them. It's much easier to get conversation flowing with fun questions, especially if your child can think some up too.

Don't be alarmed if your child gets very angry, or cries lots when they get home. The anger and tears don't necessarily mean that the day went badly. Imagine yourself starting a new job, it's been a big build-up and your first day is a little overwhelming: all the new people, new rules, new environment and expectations. You may do really well, but on the way home (or when you get home), you end up letting out everything you've been holding in all day. For your child, that anxiety, fear, stress and sheer relief, all mixed up together, can often spill out as tantrums and tears. This is natural and healthy, and while it won't last for ever, it may well last for several weeks while your child settles in. Again, meet their big emotions with calm and confident reassurance if you can; don't join them in anger or sadness.

New-found time for stay-at-home parents

I am always surprised that most starting-school articles focus solely on the child because often, the child sails through the process, while the one who struggles the most is the stay-at-home parent.

If you have spent the last four or five years at home with your child, raising and caring for them, your very identity is by now moulded around them and being their parent. Once they start school you find yourself with six hours per day that feel like a gaping hole. As your child takes a leap towards independence from you, you can almost grieve that stage in your life. It's an odd contrast: on the one hand you are immensely proud of your 'baby', for how grown up they are and for the fact that they now have a life away from you, and, on the other hand, you mourn the baby they once were and the stark realisation that you too are getting older.

Starting school is one of those rug-pull moments in parenting. You no longer know what your child is doing every minute of every day. Even if you worked prior to them starting school, you won't get an hour-by-hour rundown from their childcare provider, telling you what they did and what they ate. There is a new information hole that can leave you feeling anxious.

So what can you do if you're feeling redundant or unsure of your new role? Here are some ideas:

- **Don't be in too much of a rush to fill your time** Sit with the new-found freedom for a bit, until you figure out exactly what it is that you'd like to do with it.

- **Look for a job** The obvious thing is to get a job that fits around school hours. This is easier said than done, however – so if the right job comes along but it's full-time, don't be afraid to take it on, as long as the job excites you and you can find appropriate wraparound care.

- **Look into volunteering** If you don't want to go back to the world of work with full force (and finances allow), you could volunteer for one or two days per week. Find out what opportunities exist in your local area and visit a few to find one that feels right. Volunteering can give a real sense of purpose again, without all the commitments that a return to paid work can bring.

- **Consider a return to studying** This could mean learning a new skill at a local adult community college, or even taking on a home learning course (the Open University, for example). This can be a time to reinvent yourself and start a new learning journey, at the same time as your child.

- **Take up a sport or join a local gym or running club** Many local authorities run low-cost taster workshops you can join as part of 'get-active' schemes.

- **Take up a hobby** Either resurrect one you had that fell by the wayside when you had children or start something new. Always wanted to learn to knit? Sew? Play the guitar? Or make mosaics? Now is your chance.

- **Help out at the school** Schools are almost always desperate for parents to come in and help with listening to children read, art projects or even running lunch or after-school clubs (see Chapter 7 for more on this).

- **Think about getting a pet** This is a classic time for families to get a pet, particularly a dog, when there is time to devote to training. Having a living, breathing being in your home also helps with any displaced need to nurture and the walks will get you out of the house and give purpose to every day.

It can take at least a full term for both child and parents to fully settle, so don't be too quick to rush things. It's OK if it takes time for you all. But what if settling takes longer? Or there are many bumps along the road? The next chapter looks at some of the most common concerns of parents whose children have just started school.

Chapter 6

Common Concerns

S ome children take to school like a duck to water and parents are surprised at how easy they find the transition (especially since they usually take a lot longer to feel at ease with the change than their children). Not all children find it so easy though. Some can grapple with anxiety for many months, if not years, and others have difficulties with friendships and tricky behaviour, both at home and at school. This chapter looks at the most common concerns of parents of new school starters.

School anxiety and refusal

Perhaps the biggest concern of all is prolonged anxiety and refusal to go to school. As with anxiety before starting school, school anxiety and refusal often combine myriad different issues, packaged up under one banner. To help your child, try to unearth the real cause of their own anxiety or refusal, which may include:

- feeling overwhelmed with the size of the school, the number of children (particularly bigger ones) and all the sounds, sights and smells that go along with it

- missing you

- missing younger siblings – or jealous that they get to spend time alone with you and enjoy fun things that you may do with them

- not quite understanding what is expected of them, or what they should do and when

- being unable to find somebody to play with and sit with at lunch and break times

- feeling too stretched by the work or upset that they can't do it all easily

- not being stretched enough and feeling bored

- feeling unsettled at home for whatever reason (for instance, a new sibling arriving, moving to a new house, relationship breakdown) can mean they take extra anxiety to school, causing unsettled behaviour there

- picking up on *your* anxieties over them leaving you

- undiagnosed SEND

- undiagnosed eyesight or hearing problems

- feeling tired and not managing the transition from an exhaustion point of view

- finding difficulty with not being able to eat when they want, or with navigating lunchtimes

- personality type – for introverted children in particular.

How to handle school anxiety and refusal

Finding the underlying causes of your child's anxiety and school refusal is key to helping solve it. Working through the following tips in order can help you get to the bottom of it and, with time and patience, help to change it. Although finding the cause of the anxiety is preferable, sometimes nothing comes to light. In this case, try not to worry too much – these tips will still be applicable.

1. **Listen and observe** Find a good time to speak to your child. Often bedtime is the time they will open up the most, after you have read a story and tucked them in. This is usually a much more productive time than straight after the school run. Ask your child to think about things that make them feel sad or angry or give them an uncomfortable feeling in their tummy. Observing them is as important as what they say too, so watch what they do in the playground at drop-off and pick-up time. Do they seem to be friendly with anybody? You could also walk past at lunchtime if the school is on a public road and observe what they are doing then, or ask the teacher to make a note of what your child does at break times if you think friendship is an issue. Also, keep an eye on their sleep and eating. Are they getting enough nutrients? Certain vitamin deficiencies can increase anxiety. Is their bedtime routine good?

2. **Empathise and support** Whatever your child tells you, you should remember to validate their feelings. What they say may sound trivial to you, but it isn't to them. Don't make dismissive comments like, 'Don't be silly', or, 'You'll be OK'. This sort of toxic positivity is not helpful to them and may make them clam up and not

confide in you in the future. Similarly, don't be tempted to 'get tough'. This will make things much worse in the long run. Your child needs understanding, empathy and compassion now – not an authoritarian parent. Help your child to see that you understand and that they are safe to tell you anything without being reprimanded or belittled. Some children appreciate a hug and physical closeness for support, some prefer their own space, some like to be distracted (after the talk) with play, others prefer to just sit quietly with you. Respond in whatever way you feel is instinctively best for your child. Above all, it's important for them to know that you're on their side.

3. **Make an action plan** Once you understand the main causes behind the anxiety and refusal, together with your child, brainstorm any activities, props or plans that may help in addressing them. Request a meeting with the school and discuss your concerns and suggestions with them and ask if they have any other ideas (remember, they are very experienced at dealing with anxious and school-refusing children). Ask if you can have another meeting to review after a few days or a week as well. If friendships are an issue, ask if the school can buddy your child up with an older child who will look out for them, or if the midday assistants can create some games to get all children involved. Also, think about arranging some out-of-school playdates with children your child likes to kickstart any friendships; this is especially helpful for introverted children. If the anxiety is more related to the drop-off itself (and particularly the sensory assault that it can bring – something many children with sensory issues will find overwhelming), it may be possible to drop your child off ten minutes earlier or later than

the regular start time to avoid the chaos of the normal drop-off, which can really unsettle young children. Alternatively, is it possible to extend the settling-in period and keep your child part-time for a while? This can also help them to settle in more easily.

4. **Focus on the positives and your child's growth mindset (see page 12)** Help your child to see that it isn't school as a whole that is horrible, but only certain aspects they are struggling with, and that they won't always be unhappy there. Spend some time talking to them about what they do enjoy at school and focus on building excitement and happiness around these points. If they tell you that they don't like anything, then ask their teachers to let you know what they have enjoyed throughout the day, so that you can bring it up with them. Talk to them about their growth mindset too: it's OK that they can't do everything yet, they're still learning; but they will master things in time. Helping them to handle the disappointment of not mastering everything immediately and dialling down perfectionism a little can be very helpful.

Finally, empower your child by helping them to realise that anxiety isn't all bad – it's a sign that they care about themselves and their brain is trying to prevent them from getting into danger; the problem is that sometimes, in trying to keep us safe, our brains overreact a little and make us very fearful of situations that aren't as scary as we at first think. Help them to reframe their anxiety as a sort of magic power – a bit like their favourite superhero: it is strong because it wants to run quickly and hide or fight to protect us, but although the superhero is cool, they sometimes do the wrong thing at the wrong time. Encourage your child to talk to their anxiety superhero: they can imagine themselves shaking hands with

'Captain Anxiety' (or whatever else they want to name him or her), saying, 'It's OK, I've got this. I don't need you right now.' If your child likes drawing or painting, they can paint a picture of Captain Anxiety, so that they can picture him or her more easily and visualise saying goodbye when they need to.

5. **Check in regularly** Even if the anxiety seems short-lived, make sure that you check in with how your child is feeling regularly. School anxiety can often ebb and flow, and you may be lulled into a false sense of security once one episode has passed. Scheduling in special chats regularly can help you to keep on top of things, before they escalate. It also helps your child to feel supported and know that you are interested in how they feel, which, in turn, makes them more likely to open up to you.

6. **Provide a safe haven at home** Home should be your child's safe haven. Often school anxiety can materialise in very difficult behaviour with you. When children are at home, they should feel safe from anything that worries them at school. It should be a place for them to relax and feel comfortable enough to be themselves, so rein in a little on the discipline and take some time to work on ways to keep yourself calm. Remind yourself that they are not deliberately giving you a hard time; they are acting this way because *they* are having a hard time. This also includes focusing on your own behaviours – remember, if you are highly anxious about your child at school or not coping well with the transition, they will probably pick up on your feelings. Do whatever you need to do (and this may be more than simple self-care – speaking to a counsellor or therapist is very useful) to present that calm, confident and reassuring presence your child needs from you.

Friendship difficulties

Perhaps nothing is harder for parents than hearing their new school starter say, 'I've got nobody to play with'. Visions of them standing alone and sad, in the playground while the other children play around them are heartbreaking, but this is a common problem.

At school starting age, children are only just beginning to develop their social skills and may find it difficult to empathise with others. There is usually no malice behind excluding a child from play; it just happens. All children will have friendship problems at some point at school, but when they happen right from the start it can be far tougher to handle. So what can you do?

- **Speak to their teacher** Sometimes children say they have nobody to play with, when in reality they seem to have good relationships with others – it may be that they were alone momentarily or declined to play with anyone.

- **Does the school have strategies in place for these situations?** There may be a buddy system or an 'I'm-lonely-please-play-with-me-bench' scheme or similar. Ask the teacher how they help to support the children in forming friendships.

- **Teach your child a few icebreakers** Sometimes problems can arise because children don't know how to get involved with others' play. Teaching your child a few simple phrases such as, 'That looks like fun, can I play?' or, 'Hi, would you like to play with me?' can really help.

- **Role-play with your child** If your child has problems with social skills, then taking some time to role-play conversing with another child and joining in with their play – especially if you practise how to react to knock-backs – can empower them to act out the inter-play for real.

- **Arrange out-of-school playdates** Perhaps you could speak to a few parents in your child's class and suggest you all visit a local park after school or nip into town for a milkshake together. If your child likes one or two children in particular, then this can help to kickstart their friendship.

- **Don't push them to make friends** Often parents place too much expectation on children to form friendships quickly, and when this doesn't materialise it can hold them back and make them feel worse about their situation.

- **Remember that it's OK for them to only have one or two friends** For some parents, particularly if they're extroverts, the fact that their child has only one or two friends is considered strange. However, children can be perfectly happy with only one friend. So, as long as your child is content, there is no cause for concern, even if their friendships look very different from yours at their age.

- **Help them to manage conflict** Young children can be quite brutal when it comes to saying what they're thinking, which is rarely socially acceptable. Helping your child to know what to say if somebody is mean to them and when to walk away or get help from an adult is really important.

- **Instil positivity and confidence** Try not to meet your child's disappointment and sadness over friendships with your own. Remember the mindset theory and say, 'I know you're struggling right now, but I think you will make some good friends soon'. This is not meant to diminish what they are feeling, but to help them see that there is, hopefully, a bright side coming soon.

- **Support them at home** Friendship difficulties at school can often spill out into tricky behaviour at home. Remember, you are their safe space. Don't add to their problems.

What if you don't like your child's new friends (or their parents)?

One thing I have learned from having four children go through school is that they will be friends with whom *they* want to be friends with, and while you can try to steer them towards certain children and away from others, they will, ultimately, make their own choices. Trying to control friendships almost always ends in failure and may make them (and you) miserable; it can also have the opposite effect, in that they may gravitate more towards 'the forbidden'. Friendships at this age can be fickle and may only last a few months, or they can endure for years – it's just not possible to tell right now.

Trusting your child to make the friends who are right for them is the only way forward. Also, take the time to focus on why you are trying to control their friendships. What unconscious biases do you hold? Why don't you like a certain child? Do you need to work on your own opinions, beliefs and stereotypes? Ultimately, we all just want our children to be happy, and one of the best ways we can guarantee this is by supporting their friendship choices.

Bullying

Initially, when you hear the word bullying, you may think of physical aggression, such as hitting and kicking. However, bullying can take many forms:

- Physical violence

- Verbal teasing

- Deliberate exclusion from a group or play

- Spreading rumours (even if nothing is said directly to the child)

- Playing nasty jokes on the same child repeatedly

- Mimicking a child to others

If you suspect your child is being bullied, you must contact the school at the soonest opportunity. All schools have policies for dealing with bullying, so if you cannot find yours on their website, then call and request a copy. Make sure you keep a written log of any bullying episodes and take notes during any meetings. This paper trail and recording is important. Most schools deal swiftly and effectively with bullying, but if you don't feel it has been addressed appropriately, then your next step is to escalate the matter to the headteacher and then the board of governors. Again, putting everything in writing is important, even if you meet with them in person. (You will find a good resource for forming template letters about bullying on page 220 – see the Bullying UK website.)

Bullying is obviously very stressful for children, so do your best to stay patient and supportive with them. Help them to realise that they should always tell you what has happened, no matter what the other child or children may have said to them. Reassure them that you, as an adult, can and will help them.

From your own perspective, try to stay calm and don't be tempted to take matters into your own hands by approaching the child's parents directly. This can often cause far more problems for both you and your child. Allow the school to handle things, then follow the proper procedures to escalate and complain if they don't. The other thing you should never do is to encourage your child to hit or kick another child back or to retaliate in any other way. You may be tempted to tell them to stand up for themselves, but this doesn't usually solve anything and runs a big risk of getting your child into trouble with the school. Instead, teach them to say, 'Stop, I don't like that', and to get adult help as soon as possible.

Restraint collapse

I am often contacted by desperate parents in September or October who say, 'Help! My child has turned into a demon at home, but at school they are brilliant all day and behave really well. What have I done wrong?' The presumption here is that the parents must be at fault because the school isn't having the same issue that they are at home. And in a sense this is true – but not in a negative way. In fact, these parents are doing everything right – because when you make your child feel loved, safe, supported and respected at home, they feel comfortable enough to be their authentic selves with you. In other words, they don't have to pretend or 'be good'.

Children spend all day at school, holding in frustration, fear, anxiety, anger and other uncomfortable emotions because they know that it is 'naughty' to let them out there. But when they get home things are entirely different. There is a massive release. Imagine your child at school as a bottle of fizzy drink: all day they are being shaken, building pressure, but they manage to 'be good' and keep their lid screwed on tightly. When they see you, the need to release is huge, and pop – off comes the lid and the ensuing spray of all that has been bottled up inside. The technical term for this is restraint collapse, but I much prefer to think of it in terms of that bottle finally releasing its pressure. This is all very complimentary of your parenting skills; if you hadn't made your child feel secure enough to be authentic with you, when they were feeling happy or otherwise, then they would continue to bottle up the feelings and the release (and subsequent mess) would be more likely to happen at school, causing far more problems.

Many children get into the cycle of not being able to release to their parents – perhaps because they have been raised to not share how they feel through constant punishments and exclusions, or perhaps because the parents have been too busy to listen, or absent. The result then is constant difficulty and poor behaviour at school, as they try to keep a lid on things and erratically explode outside the safety of home.

What can you do about restraint collapse? The best thing is to understand and accept it for what it is: a great testament to the hard work you have put into raising a child with good emotional intelligence and a strong bond with you. The effects wear off as children settle into school and things become easier for them, but it will rear its head time and again throughout the school years. When it happens again (after initially ceasing) you will know that something is wrong at school. Don't take any explosions personally. They are definitely not acting this way because they hate you; it's actually a bizarre way of them saying that they love you, lots. Instead, let your child know that it's OK, you're here for them and you're big enough and mature enough to hold their difficult feelings as well as their happy ones.

Restraint collapse can last a lot longer than most parents imagine. It's not uncommon for elements to continue throughout your child's time at school, well into their teen years. Coping with it in the long term is no different from coping with it in the short term: understand that it is normal and common; be your child's safe place, try to stay calm and remind yourself that they are not behaving this way on purpose.

Regression of behaviour at home

As well as restraint collapse, it's very common for three specific behaviours to regress once children start school. These are: eating, toileting and sleep. These are the only three aspects of their lives that children have full control over; as such, they are often the ones that nosedive during tricky transitions.

Eating

Before starting school, most children have much more control over their eating in that they can snack and graze throughout the day. Once they start school, they are limited to eating either only at lunchtime or at lunch and at one break time (a small snack). Some children can struggle with this restriction and can show signs of hanger (hunger manifesting as anger); others eat so much at lunchtime that they have no appetite for any food once they get home; and still others eat very little at school, so are ravenous when they get home. The best response here is to follow your child's lead. If they are adamant that they are not hungry, trust that they know their own body. If they are certain that they need more to eat, then listen to them. Hunger seems to particularly strike at the end of the school day, so I always tried to take a snack with me on the school run, as my children were in much better moods if they had the offer of food almost as soon as the school day finished.

Toileting

Toileting regressions are also not uncommon. Wetting and soiling occur with regularity in the first year or two of school, and your child certainly won't be the only one doing it. But why does this happen?

In the first few weeks and months when children are settling in and getting to know the school and staff, they can be too nervous or embarrassed to ask to go to the toilet, or they may forget where they are or simply be so engrossed in what they're doing that they leave going to the toilet too late. School toilets also create a certain amount of anxiety for many children, who don't like the lack of privacy, with gaps between the doors and no soundproofing. It's common for schoolchildren to be 'shy pooers' and to do everything within their power to avoid doing it at school. This can cause soiling accidents or sometimes constipation as they try to hold on throughout the day. Some children also drink far less throughout the school day than they do at home (despite having access to water most of the day), which can cause constipation. Constipation can, in turn, lead to diarrhoea and 'overflow poo', where runny poo seeps out around the sides of a solid blockage. If your child is affected by any of these things, speak to their teacher and ask for suggestions. They will have dealt with this sort of thing many times before.

Sleep

Sleep regressions are also common among new school starters. Any transition or event that makes us feel nervous, anxious, scared or stressed impacts on our sleep as adults, and the same is true for children. As discussed earlier, children need time to unwind and reconnect with their parents at the end of the school day. Trying to rush them into their bedtime routine too soon, with a bedtime that is too early, can cause children to be sleep deprived, as their bodies are too full of cortisol to relax. This means that they end up going to sleep far later or they have a very disrupted night. If sleep regression is an issue when your child starts school, I would recommend that you reread the information on this on pages 107–10.

Behaviour Regression in School Holidays

Tantrums, tears, aggression, hyperactivity, sulks and other unpredictable behaviour during the school holidays are often a concentrated form of restraint collapse. There is definitely an element of your child letting all their emotions out during the weeks at home with you, after holding them in for a school term. There are other causes of difficult behaviour in the holidays too though.

The first is related to sleep, which will often nosedive during school holidays, with bedtime routines and boundaries slipping. Children are commonly allowed to stay up later in the holidays, and with lots of travel and days out, bedtime routines can fall by the wayside. Always try to keep both bedtime and wake time consistent over school holidays. Similarly, bedtime routines are as important as ever, so avoid letting them slip just because there is no school for a while.

However, the main cause of behaviour regression during school holidays is the lack of daily routine. By the time the first half-term break comes along, the new school patterns have become a solid part of your child's life. They know when to expect to wake up and go to bed, to get dressed, brush their teeth and their hair, have food and so on. Then, along comes a school holiday and everything they know suddenly goes out the window. They can no longer predict anything. The lax routines that school holidays bring – that perhaps you think give them time to chill and relax – can cause them to feel insecure and confused. So difficult behaviour is often a pushback to these feelings of uncertainty and a perceived lack of control. The simple way to resolve this is to keep a routine going throughout the holiday, with regular wake-up and bedtimes, food times and so on. And the added bonus here is that you won't have to battle with trying to get them back into routine again at the end of the school holiday.

Of course, it can be hard to keep a routine going if you are away, but the more you try to incorporate elements of your regular daily life, the less difficult the transition will be for your child, which usually means much better behaviour and, therefore, a more enjoyable holiday for all.

Tiredness after school and on waking in the morning

The first few months at school can be exhausting, not just for children, but for parents too, as they carry the strain of the emotional transitions, leaving them feeling burned-out.

Children can often suffer from tiredness, resulting in tricky mornings, when they just don't want to get out of bed and difficult evenings, when they fall asleep the minute you get them home from school, making bedtime hard (or when they don't fall asleep the minute you get them home and their resulting mood makes the rest of the evening feel impossible). All of this usually passes fairly quickly, within a term or two at most, once children get used to the new activities and their circadian rhythms (body clocks) reset to the new timings. Until then, focus on creating some calming activities at home – don't worry too much about TV time for an hour or two when they get in from the school run and avoid after-school activities and clubs.

If the tiredness continues into the new year, then it would be worth checking if there are any underlying medical causes, such as mineral deficiencies, and speaking to the school about the possibility of reducing your child's hours there temporarily to help them adjust, especially if they are not yet five years old.

Ensuring your child is appropriately challenged

Children who are struggling or who are bored at school can often be misunderstood and thought of as being difficult or naughty, when there is actually an educational need underlying their behaviour. This should, ideally, be picked up on by the child's teacher who should be able to tailor their teaching to suit children over a wide variety of abilities. However, sometimes children are missed. If you suspect that this is the case with your child, your first port of call should always be a chat with their teacher. Raise your concerns and ask what they can do to support or stretch your child more and if there is anything you can do at home to help. If they do not allay your concerns, or you find that there is no improvement after you have spoken to them, then your next step would be to request a meeting with the headteacher.

Undiagnosed SEND

Many children with special educational needs (ADHD, dyslexia, dyspraxia, sensory processing disorder, for example) will enter school undiagnosed. Parents may have a niggling suspicion that they are a little different in some way during the toddler and preschool years, but it's only when they start school that the gulf seems to widen.

Frustratingly, SEND is underbudgeted almost universally. There is just not enough awareness, training, diagnoses or, most importantly, support available. For some, the path to diagnosis and then putting support into place can be frustratingly long. I write this not only from the perspective of a professional, but as the mother of a son with ADHD who was not diagnosed until secondary school, despite the fact that I knew there was something different about him from the age of two years.

The first hurdle is finding somebody to listen to your concerns. That may be the school's SENCo (special educational needs coordinator), the school nurse or, in our case, the family doctor. If your fears are dismissed and you still feel that something is not right, don't give up. Seek a second, third and fourth opinion. Be your child's advocate and be prepared to stand up and be heard – for them. It shouldn't be this difficult of course, and often it isn't, but children with undiagnosed SEND can all too often get lost in the school system or be dismissed as simply immature or 'naughty'. The best advice I can give you here is to listen to your gut; your instinct won't be wrong. If you feel that the school are not supportive enough, then ask for help from your doctors or see if there are any child emotional-health organisations you can refer to locally. Finally, seek support from other parents who have been through similar. There are more and more virtual communities now, if you don't manage to find one locally, and they can make all the difference to you, as being the parent of a child with SEND (particularly an undiagnosed one) can be a very lonely place.

Can you change school or de-register if it's really not working?

However tricky your child (and you) may be finding school right now, it is almost always possible to resolve whatever issue you are facing, with the support of the school and a little time and patience. But if you have reason to believe that your choice of school was a horrible mistake and you are certain that you don't want them to stay there, you have two options:

1. **Changing schools** This is known as an 'in-year admission' and will be dealt with differently, depending on where you live. Some schools (such as private schools, free schools and academies) will handle their own in year admissions; others (mostly maintained schools) may be controlled by your local authority. If you are thinking of changing schools, you should first find out from your local authority whether you need to apply via them or directly to the school you are interested in. Next, contact the schools you would consider and ask if they have any current vacancies. If they do, you can request to meet with them for a visit and ask them the questions covered earlier (see Chapter 2). Once you've decided on a school, you will need to apply, either directly or through the

local authority, and when you've been awarded a place, get in touch with the headteacher to make arrangements for a starting date and settling-in procedure. The same applies if you find yourself moving to a different area after your child starts school.

2. **De-registering** Perhaps you don't feel that your child is suited to school at the moment; maybe they are not yet compulsory school age and you have decided you now want to keep them at home with you until they are; or perhaps you feel that school is not a good fit with your child full stop. In these cases, you may think about taking them out of school and home-educating (if you live in a country where it is legal). If your child is not of compulsory school age, then the process is usually less formal, with a simple notification of de-registering given to the school, usually in a short, written form. If your child is of compulsory school age and attending a regular (not special needs) state or private school, then you should write to the headteacher to inform them that you will be de-registering. You do not have to discuss this with the school, even if they request a meeting with you, and they do not have authority to deny the de-registration either (again, assuming home-education is legal where you live). It is a good idea to get confirmation of receipt of this letter or send a hard copy via recorded delivery as proof of notification. This is important in case you are accused of truancy and a fine is issued for non-attendance and you need to produce evidence that the school was indeed informed of your intent to de-register. The headteacher, in turn, must legally inform your local authority. You will find some home-education resources on page 219 to guide you through the process of de-registering and setting up home-education.

Concerns around demands from school

While many of the concerns that crop up during the first year of school are centred around your child, and how they settle in – or not – others have more to do with you, as parents, particularly when it comes to coping with the financial and time pressures placed on you by the school.

Requests for parental input

Very soon after your child starts school, you'll start receiving requests for various items to be sent in: harvest food parcel contents, festive play costumes, objects for project work, empty containers for junk modelling, Victorian schoolchildren outfits, World Book Day dressing up, food for end-of-term celebrations and specific coloured T-shirts for sports days. As a new school parent, it can be tempting to throw your all into all of these requests, and there is nothing wrong with this, as long as your finances and time allow. If you are pushed for time and money, though, don't enter into the mythical 'good-parent' sweepstakes by worrying about whether you send in something homemade or a shop-bought alternative.

After putting four children through school, I quickly realised that borrowing from friends, social-media second-hand sites, charity shops and Amazon Prime were the way forward. Believe me, nobody is judging what sort of a parent you are by whether your child is wearing a supermarket or home-sewn star costume. Others will be just as likely to be concerned about whether their Mr Kipling cakes will be noticed in the school bake-sale donations as you are about your hastily thrown-together Rice Krispie traybake. What matters is that your child is happy. And I've realised that children are just as happy in a pillowcase with holes cut out for the head and arms and a bit of tinsel wrapped around their heads as they are in an all-singing, all-dancing, light-up gold lamé angel costume.

One final note here, never throw these things away once they've been used: if you have younger children, they will most likely need the same things a year or more down the line; and if you don't need them, the school will probably be very grateful for donations, as are other parents on social-media free giveaway sites.

Requests for money

This is a tough one. My children have all attended state schools and I have been constantly surprised at how much we have had to pay out for different school trips, activities, special equipment and the like. And that's without factoring in the sponsorship requests and the small fortune you end up spending at school fetes. I found that saving a little each month (via a direct debit) helped to spread the cost throughout the year, rather than having to face unexpected bills when the money had run out at the end of the month. I would also sell outgrown uniforms to try to recoup some money (and buy the next size up second-hand if I could).

If you are really suffering from the financial demands of school, speak to the head, in confidence. Schools are often able to offer financial assistance through special schemes and funds, although these may have to be requested. There are also likely to be local charities that can help in some way too – again, their existence is not usually common knowledge though.

Finally, make sure that you know whether the school is requesting a donation, or if the payment is mandatory – sometimes there can be confusion over the two. Although I would always advocate donating a payment if you can do so (because school budgets are stretched to the limit too), you do not need to put yourself into financial difficulty if the payment is not mandatory. Similarly, the school is not allowed to chase you or exclude your child from an activity if the payment requested is only a donation. Do read the wording of letters carefully to spot the difference – and ask, if you are uncertain.

Common parasites and illnesses at school

Because of the close proximity of the children to each other and their less than ideal personal care, viruses, bugs and unwanted visitors can spread like wildfire. Here are some of the most common ones along with some tips on how to deal with them and reduce the chances that they will reappear.

Worms

Threadworms, sometimes known as pinworms, are common in the early years of school. They are very fine (like thick cotton thread) and white and are usually between 5mm and 1cm long. They can live for just over a month in the gut and reproduce by laying eggs around the anus. Eggs can live for up to two weeks outside the body and reinfection is common, when children scratch their anus, lodging the eggs under their fingernails and then put their fingers into their mouths, thus starting the cycle again. It is usual for all members of a family to catch worms, because of the eggs surviving outside the body and being passed by touch or infected towels and so on.

Symptoms

- Interrupted sleep

- Itching around the anus and vagina, especially at night in bed.

- Appearance of worms around the anus at night

- Irritability (usually because of the poor sleep)

- Teeth grinding

- Bedwetting

Treatment

The main treatment for worms is known as mebendazole (although it will usually have a trade name) and is available at pharmacies in tablet or liquid form. (You do not need to see a doctor to purchase it.) It works by starving the threadworms of the sugar they need to survive. All family members should be treated, even if they are asymptomatic. Two doses are needed: the first, to kill the existing adult worms and the second (around two weeks later), to kill those that are newly hatched. Children do not usually need to stay off school if they have worms.

Prevention

Preventing reinfection is vital, as the medicine does not kill the eggs: keep nails short, wash all towels, bedding and under-wear regularly on a hot wash and don't share them among family members. Shower daily, paying particular attention to cleaning around the anus, and make sure everybody washes their hands before eating, preferably scrubbing underneath fingernails. Finally, it's a good idea for infected children to wear underwear at night to inhibit scratching and any spread to bedclothes.

Head lice

Head lice are prevalent among younger schoolchildren and the chances of your child making it through school without at least one bout are very small. Head lice are caught by a child's head being in close proximity to the head of another child who has lice. Given how young children sit and play very near to each other, it's no surprise that lice are passed on so easily. Head lice do not discriminate between clean and dirty hair and are not, therefore, an indication that a child is unclean. They are small insects which grow to up to half a centimetre long. Their colour varies between pale brown and black. They lay eggs, known as nits, which are brown when they contain a louse, or white when they are empty.

Symptoms

- Itchy scalp

- Crawling sensation over the scalp

- Poor sleep (with lots of head scratching)

- Irritability (due to the poor sleep)

- Visible lice and nits in the hair and scalp

Treatment

Perhaps when you were at school you were visited by the 'nit nurse', who would check through your hair regularly for the presence of lice. Sadly, this service no longer exists, so it is up to parents to look for and treat lice when they appear.

Head lice can be treated at home and you do not need to see a doctor. Your child also does not need to stay off school during the treatment. There are various treatment options for headlice:

- **Wet combing** Usually done using a special metal 'nit comb' while the hair is coated in conditioner, to pull out both the lice and nits. This should be performed every other day for at least seventeen days, until the combing does not draw out any lice or nits. This is by far the most popular treatment option and usually the most successful.

- **Medicated lotions** Purchased from online retailers, supermarkets and pharmacies, these work to kill the live lice, so treatment needs to be repeated to ensure the newly hatched lice are killed. They can be expensive and their efficacy is not always great.

- **Electronic combs** These work in a similar way to the metal combs used for wet combing, only they also deliver a small electrical pulse to kill any lice they detect. However, they are expensive and not really any more effective than a regular nit comb.

All members of the family should be checked and treated for headlice if a child is infected.

Prevention

Although it is almost impossible to prevent head lice, the following may help to reduce recurrence:

- Tie long hair back, braided if possible.

- Use a repellent spray or oil daily, such as tea tree or neem.

- Comb weekly prophylactically with a nit comb, even if no active infestation is present.

Hand-foot-and-mouth disease (HFMD)

HFMD (or, to give it its proper name, coxsackievirus) is a common childhood virus with a duration of seven to ten days. Despite the name, it is unrelated to the animal variety of foot-and-mouth disease. HFMD is spread via bodily fluids, such as saliva.

Symptoms

- Fever

- Sore throat

- Refusing to eat

- Mouth ulcers (appearing a few days after the above)

- Red spots all over the body, which turn into blisters with a grey centre (appearing a few days after the above).

Treatment

If your child is not immunocompromised and you are sure that they have HFMD, then there is no need to visit your doctor.* Treatment is simply to keep the child happy and comfortable, with pain relief, lots of fluids and easy-to-eat, soft food. Children should stay off school until the fever has gone (usually the first two days).

*Note: if you are in any doubt as to the cause of your child's rash, please do seek professional medical advice.

Slapped-cheek syndrome

Slapped-cheek syndrome (or fifth disease or Parvovirus B19, as it is known medically) is a common childhood illness that lasts for around two weeks. The virus is spread by saliva and mucous and a child is only infectious before the rash appears, hence why it spreads so easily – because most parents do not know their child has it at the point when they are infectious.

Symptoms

- Fever

- Sore throat

- Runny nose

- Headache

- A bright red rash on the cheeks (giving the appearance of having been slapped, hence the name); this appears a day or two after the above

- Following the above, a pink, raised, itchy rash may appear over the rest of the body.

Treatment

If your child is not immunocompromised and you are sure that they have slapped-cheek, then there is no need to visit your doctor.* Treatment is just to keep them happy and comfortable, with pain relief, lots of fluids and easy-to-eat, soft food and a cooling lotion to help reduce itchiness. As they are no longer contagious once the rash appears, there is no need to keep children off school if they do not feel unwell.

*Note: if you are in any doubt as to the cause of your child's rash, please do seek professional medical advice.

Chickenpox

Chickenpox is caused by the varicella zoster virus. A child is infectious from two days before the first spots appear and until they have all crusted over, which usually takes around five days. It is spread very easily – just by being in the same room as another infected child or by touching items they have touched.

Symptoms

- Fever

- Generalised aches and pains

- Irritability

- Loss of appetite

- A rash that starts with red spots, which then become fluid-filled blisters before scabbing over a few days after appearing.

Treatment

If your child is not immunocompromised and you are sure they have chickenpox, then there is no need to visit your doctor.* You will need to keep them off school until the last spot has scabbed over. Treatment is just to keep the child happy and comfortable, with pain relief (but not ibuprofen, which can cause dangerous skin infections when given to a child with chickenpox), lots of fluids and easy-to-eat, soft food and a cooling lotion to help to reduce itchiness.

*Note: if you are in any doubt as to the cause of your child's rash, please do seek professional medical advice.

Tummy bugs

Tummy bugs are incredibly common at school, with viruses being spread through body fluids. As young children are not known for their personal hygiene, including hand-washing, it is likely that once one child has a bug, it will spread quickly around the rest of the class.

Symptoms

- Diarrhoea

- Vomiting

Treatment

If your child is infected, keep them comfortable with lots of fluids and plain foods. Following BRAT is a good way to remember the foods they may be able to tolerate:

- **Bananas**

- **Rice**

- **Apples**

- **Toast**

You can also buy rehydration salts from pharmacies to replace lost electrolytes and help your child to feel better more quickly. Schools will usually have a policy whereby children need to remain home from school for at least forty-eight hours following the last vomiting or diarrhoea episode, even if they are otherwise well.

Coughs and colds

Coughs and colds are very common at school and very easily spread. There is no need to keep your child at home unless they are feeling very bad and otherwise unable to be at school – for instance if they have a fever or are in a lot of pain.

'Mental-health days'

What if your child doesn't have a specific illness but they have days when they really don't want to go to school – perhaps because they feel tired or they just need a break? As adults, we certainly appreciate a day hibernating and relaxing every now and again, so why should it be any different for children? I firmly believe that they should be able to stay home in these instances if at all possible (of course, this is not so easy for you if you work and don't have alternative childcare). I allow my children to have one 'mental-health day' (as I call them) per term. People say to me, 'But don't they always try to skip school if you let them do this?' to which my answer is, 'No. Because they know that I am trusting them and that I expect honesty in return.' They also know that they are not allowed more than one of these days per term – that is a firm boundary and they rarely try to test it.

I find that mental-health days can help to reset the child's motivation and happiness levels. They tend to go back to school with a much better attitude, which is a positive for me, them and the school.

When informing the school of a mental-health day I have

always simply said that my child is sick. If they press further, then I will say that they are feeling very tired, anxious or emotionally run down. I have never had the legitimacy of this questioned and always make sure that they attend school normally, aside from serious illnesses, so their attendance is otherwise good, which I think is key to the school's acceptance of it.

It's not possible to cover every eventuality here, but I hope this chapter has helped with some of the concerns you may experience over the first year of school. The underlying theme is always to have good, open communication with the school. It is much easier to resolve things together than it is alone. The next chapter will focus more on this relationship – the one between you and the whole school community – and how you can make it as positive as possible.

Chapter 7

The School Community and You

When children start school for the first time, most of the emphasis when it comes to preparation and settling in is from the child's perspective only. However, the way in which parents and carers relate to the school staff and community as a whole is just as important to the child's happiness and success there. Sometimes more so. An engaged parent or carer, who works to form a good relationship with the school and supports the staff with their child's learning, will almost always have children who are happier and higher-achieving than those whose parents remain detached.

With at least twelve years of raising a school child ahead of you, it makes sense that you try to enjoy the experience as much as possible for your own benefit too. School is going to play a huge part in your life, as well as your child's. It will take up a large chunk of your social life and free time, outside of school hours, you will make new friends, just as your child does and you will need a support network of similar-minded parents you can turn to at nine o'clock at night, when you realise you've forgotten to provide a Roman soldier costume for the next morning, or when an important appointment means you can't drop your child off at the school disco. Does this mean you have to throw yourself in at the deep end and eat, sleep and breathe school or raise thousands for the PTA? Of course not (unless you want to) – but it does mean that your relationship with the school and those involved with it matters. This chapter covers the ways in which you can build on that relationship and make it as positive as possible for yourself, the school and your child, including when you disagree with the way things are done.

Building a good relationship with the school

The following are important in forming the basis of a positive school–parent relationship:

- **Good, open communication** There should be clear guidelines for how to best contact your child's teacher, support staff, leadership team and any governors and when, where and how to direct queries and worries. Similarly, school staff should foster open communication with parents, not just at parents' evenings and report times, but on a more frequent basis, especially if they have any concerns. Parents, in turn, should impart information that they feel is important to share with the school in a respectful way.

- **Mutual respect** An ideal school community will involve parents who respect the teachers and the work that they do, as well as other members of school staff. And vice versa too – school staff should display respect towards parents, with both groups respecting the children.

- **Understanding and empathy** Parents can often become frustrated with the schooling system in general but misdirect their frustration towards teachers. The most common issues that parents face and disagree with (such as classroom behaviour management, time spent on certain subjects rather than others and testing) are firmly rooted at a governmental level. As the face of education, however, teachers become the fall guys for complaints and grievances (even though they probably agree with the views of the parents most of the time, but can't be seen to do so publicly). The sad reality is that education is underfunded and undervalued, with teachers being overworked and underpaid. It can be so helpful if parents differentiate between their overall frustration at the system as a whole and concerns about what teachers are doing that can be changed. Similarly, many school workers would do well to remember that parents are probably already doing the best they can and they shouldn't expect them to resolve all behaviour issues that happen at school; instead, they should take some responsibility and appreciate that parents can do very little about what their children do when they are not with them.

- **Co-operation and collaboration** Working collaboratively with a good level of involvement from both school and parents or carers, particularly if your child is struggling with their behaviour, is the only way to change things effectively. The best education happens when parents are actively and positively involved with the teachers and vice versa.

What if you disagree with school discipline policies?

If you have read *The Gentle Discipline Book*, you will be well aware that I disagree with most mainstream school behaviour-control methods, which focus heavily on rewards (headteacher certificates, 'Star of the Week', star charts, 'Golden Time', behaviour traffic-light charts, house points and Dojo points – another version of house points) and punishments (time out, missing break times and school celebrations). The problem with these methods is that any change to behaviour is superficial. A child who is rewarded to behave well, or punished when they behave badly, is not making any deep change to the way they think and feel, thus there will be no long-lasting positive change to their behaviour.

By focusing on external manipulation of behaviour (or extrinsic motivation) via the use of rewards or punishments, you ignore the internal drivers of behaviour (or intrinsic motivation). This emphasis on artificial control of behaviour, with metaphorical carrots and sticks, is not only deeply ineffective long-term, but can really damage a child's intrinsic drive to behave and do well at school. Perhaps most importantly of all, these methods do nothing to identify or help the child to solve the problem underlying their difficult behaviour. At best, mainstream school discipline is crowd control in an understaffed, overstretched classroom.

What schools need to do is to shift the focus away from motivating and demotivating children to behave in a certain way. They need to scrap the rewards, punishments and outdated behaviourist approaches and to focus instead on building honest and open relationships with children, where there is no fear of retribution. They need to ask why, how and what: *why* is this child not thriving at school? *How* is the child feeling? And *what* do they need in order to thrive? What unmet needs does the child have that are causing the problems? Do they have an undiagnosed SEND? Are they struggling with friendships, bullying or anxiety? There is always an underlying 'What?' and if it isn't identified and worked with, it will only continue to grow.

Most school discipline punishes children for having a problem, rather than helping them to solve it. The difficulty is that the individual approach to behaviour management that is so sorely needed takes more time than simply sending a child to red on the traffic-light display, or making them sit outside the headteacher's office. It requires a bespoke solution for each and every problem. And schools just don't have the time or the resources to do this. This is ironic and deeply sad, considering that switching to a more collaborative, restorative behaviour-management practice would save both money and time in the long run.

So what can you do? Here are five important points to work with:

1. **Come from a position of understanding** Remember to approach any discussions with teachers with the respect, understanding, empathy, collaboration and open and honest communication mentioned at the start of this chapter. And keep your goals realistic, bearing in mind the limitations faced by the school. They are not going to change their whole approach to discipline based on your discussion, but they may agree to look at one very small aspect of it. So pick your battles, going for whatever it is that bothers you the most, rather than trying to change the world all at once.

2. **Be your child's advocate** Be prepared to stand up for your child and their rights, even when you feel uncomfortable

doing so. They need you to be their voice and in their corner. Always approach discussions with the school as a team with them.

3. **Your child's class teacher should always be your first port of call** If you still have concerns after speaking to them, however, the next step is to request a meeting with the headteacher. Of, if your concerns are about SEND (or potentially), ask to meet the school's SENCo. Make sure you write down your worries before heading into the meeting, and take notes while you are in there. You could also follow this meeting up with an email, detailing the key points discussed and asking for a printout to be placed in your child's file. Emails create paper trails that are much harder to ignore.

4. **Consider joining your school's board of governors** Sometimes it is easier to petition for change from the inside.

5. **Think about how you can ameliorate any negative impact at home** At the start of this book, I explained that you were – and always will be – the most important influence on your child. They are resilient, but you can make them more so. If you focus on unconditional support at home and act as your child's sounding board and champion, then a few days on a sad cloud or red traffic light or a handful of superficial certificates really will have a negligible effect. Discuss how a certificate made your child feel. Ask if they felt proud, then say, 'Ah, we don't need certificates to show that, do we? It's what we feel inside that matters the most and I'm *always* proud of you.' Teach them to feel pride in their efforts, as well as their accomplishments, and help them to realise that they are always safe to discharge their difficult emotions with you at home. You can also discuss why schools need to use behavioural-control methods that

you don't use at home, explaining that because there are so many children to care for they have to do things you don't use or agree with at home.

Ultimately, you have very little say in how schools do things, but you have total control over what you do at home, and that is always far more important.

While I am happy to compromise on most forms of school discipline, there are two that I cannot ever support: attendance awards and clean-plate certificates.

It is ludicrous to award children for a high attendance rate (usually in the region of 98–100 per cent), thereby punishing those whose attendance, for whatever reason, is less good. Children have no control over whether they are sick, or if their parents find it hard, for whatever reason, to get them into school or if there any other issues that may prevent them attending. Effectively punishing a child who has a chronic health condition, requiring multiple medical appointments, one who has been unlucky enough to contract several infectious illnesses in a term or one whose parents are separating, experiencing financial problems or have health issues of their own is short-sighted at best. These schemes do far more harm than good and they should be stopped.

The other form of school discipline for which I have zero tolerance is reward stickers or certificates for 'eating well' or clearing dinner plates. These awards encourage overeating and non-mindful eating, which, as children grow, can turn into severe eating disorders and obesity. My daughter once left school with an 'I-ate-all-my-lunch-up-today' sticker and I immediately asked the school never to reward (or punish or chastise) her for her eating again. I don't think they realised just how damaging one little sticker could be until I explained it to them. Thankfully, I never saw any eating-related stickers or certificates after our discussion.

Joining the parent–teacher association (PTA)

Joining the PTA can be a wonderful way to make new friends and to get to know other parents and teachers at the school quickly, as well as making a positive difference to your child's school. It can also be a good way to fill some time and feel needed again, if you are feeling a little lost and bereft after your child has started school.

Your time commitment to the PTA can be as much or as little as you can spare, so don't be put off joining if you work full-time. Equally, don't feel guilty if you don't join in right away because you need to find your feet and balance your time between work and school. Most PTAs will just be terribly grateful for whatever help you can offer, whether that is attending every meeting and co-arranging the school's summer fete or donating items for a fundraising raffle. Attending PTA meetings is, however, a great way to get to know not only the parents of children in the same year as yours, but those with older children too. These more experienced school parents, whom you might not otherwise come across, can be a wealth of information.

For most parents, joining the PTA gives them and their family much more than they need to give back.

Volunteering as a parent helper

Volunteering your time in the classroom can help to forge bonds with the school and give you a real fly-on-the-wall view of what happens there. An added advantage is that your child will love seeing you around the building.

Most schools are more than happy for parents to help out with listening to children read, chaperoning on school trips, assisting at lunchtime and after-school clubs and lending any relevant professional skills they may have for a special lesson or two. You will need to be police checked, to ensure the children's safety and meet the school's insurance requirements, but this is quick and easy to organise.

The best way to approach the idea of volunteering is to have a chat with your child's teacher a few weeks into the school term, once things have settled a little and staff have time to talk to you and make the necessary arrangements.

A year of firsts

Your child's first year at school will bring many firsts, not just for them, but for you too. Parents evenings, school reports, school trips, sports day and school plays are just some of the events that you will be experiencing for the first time as a parent, and this section covers the most important points to be aware of in order to get the most out of them.

Parents' evening

Most schools will run at least one parents' evening each year, and often there will be two or three. Parents' evenings are a chance for you to talk to your child's teacher in more depth than a quick playground chat allows. Most appointments are around ten to twenty minutes long. You will also be able to see examples of your child's work and may get to look around their classroom.

Parents' evenings shouldn't bring any surprises. If your child is struggling, then you should have been made aware of this as soon as possible; similarly, don't wait until parents' evening to raise any of your own concerns. These meetings should just focus on what your child is doing well and give you a chance chat about little niggles or worries, rather than big issues. The arrangement of parents' evenings will vary between schools. Some will offer an online booking system; some will ask you to sign up on a sheet of paper. And some schools will ask that only parents attend, while others will be happy for children to be there too.

School reports

School reports are generally distributed yearly in the early years of school, usually at the end of the school year. These written reports will contain an in-depth observation of your child's strengths and areas that they need to work on. Again, they should focus on positives, rather than negatives and any issues should have been discussed long before their release, so that there are no unhappy surprises.

Some reports will include statistical data giving an idea of where your child sits within expectations for their age and national averages. Do try not to get too hung up on these – they don't tell you anything about your child's happiness or wellbeing and they don't predict the future; they are a very narrow measurement of a specific period of time and shouldn't be treated as anything more.

Many schools also operate scrapbook systems (either online or hard-copy) in order to keep in touch with parents on a weekly basis, allowing you to upload photos and information about your child's week and achievements at home and view pictures and notes from the teachers about your child's time at school. The rising use at school of internet-based technology is making this sort of reporting more common, enabling real-time feedback to parents. If your school doesn't use this system already, then do ask if they plan to in the future.

School trips

The first school trip can be a daunting experience for new school parents. For many, this is the first time that their children have travelled without them or with somebody who isn't close family. It is common and normal to be nervous and anxious. I remember clearly the first few trips my children went on and how I spent all day worrying about the coach crashing. I thought I was insane until I spoke to some other mothers at the school pick-up that day who all confessed to having felt exactly the same. I found that the best way to reassure myself was to ask questions: how experienced is the driver? What safety measures are there on board? Who will be caring for the children? What time do they plan to arrive? There really are no silly questions, so don't be afraid to ask. Asking questions is also important so that you can prepare your child, especially if they are anxious. I also found it helpful to speak to parents with children in older classes and ask about their experiences with the trip.

Plays, sports day and assemblies

School plays, assemblies and sports days have changed little from your own childhood. They are a rite of passage and hopefully something that will remain unchanged for many years. Of course, there are a few differences, the most significant I've noted being the following:

- School plays and assemblies now tend to be ticketed (and if you don't have a ticket, you don't get in). Often sales are restricted to only two per child, meaning siblings and grandparents can't attend. Of course, if siblings aren't permitted, this can also present logistical problems in terms of childcare; my husband and I used to have to take it in turns to attend school productions, with one of us remaining at home with the other children. Not ideal.

- Sports days are mostly non-competitive. Gone are the awards for first, second and third place, and in their place are 'growth-mindset' certificates and 'kindest-team' awards. This seems like growth-mindset theory taken to the extreme, way beyond anything that Carol Dweck (founder of the theory) ever intended, but it does seem to avoid some of the tears and meltdowns of years gone by.

- In today's online society, parents no longer have full control over who sees their child's image, while schools have to seriously worry about photographs and videos of children being shared on social media. Most schools therefore now have a no-photographs-or-video policy at school events, including assemblies. This can initially seem silly and irritating, but the rule is in place solely for the protection of the children. Even if you don't mind your own child's face popping up on somebody else's social-media account, there may be a child who needs to be kept off for safeguarding reasons. The only way to protect all children is to impose strict guidelines or even a total ban.

Teacher gifts and tokens of appreciation

If you look at any online-parent forum in late June or early July, you will see endless messages asking, 'What are your best ideas for end-of-year teacher gifts?' The annual tradition of gift-giving to teachers when your child is about to graduate from their class (and sometimes at festivals, such as Christmas) still holds strong. This means every year teachers are inundated with more mugs than they can ever hope to use in their life-time. Do you need to give a gift? Absolutely not. Teachers don't expect them, and although they can be incredibly touched by gestures of gratitude, a handwritten note can be valued just as much as an expensive gift, if not more so. If you do want to give a gift, however, smaller, personalised and more thoughtful items tend to be the most appreciated, as highlighted in some of the responses I received when asking teachers about their favourite gifts from students and parents:

A handwritten card from the parents. I've kept all the cards with a thoughtful message in!

My favourite gifts I have kept, were a small vase decorated by a five-year-old (it was filled with chocolate). Also, a hand-drawn picture of a child I taught and me in a frame the child had decorated. I also have kept and treasured a keyring a ten-year-old made for me. It's definitely the pupil input that makes a gift special.

I absolutely love gifts I can make use of, like stationery and Post-it notes.

I really appreciated getting a coffee shop gift card once; it isn't something I usually spend money on, so it was a real luxury.

Last year I was given a personalised canvas bag that was lovely and very useful (it says, 'Mrs X's bag of books').

Things that say the teacher's name that are useful for the job like book bags or notebooks and stationery always seemed to be kept and used by teachers I worked with as well.

Coffee! After teaching for many years, I really don't need or want any 'teacher mugs' or anything along those lines. I have to donate a lot of them eventually because my cabinets start overflowing. Coffee is always welcome though.

My favourite present was from a class who made a picture out of buttons on a canvas, which they had all signed with thank-you messages. It still hangs on my wall.

Boxes of biscuits are always welcome; they are kept for the whole school staff to munch on during meetings.

A box of chocolates for the staffroom, so everyone can benefit.

Anything handmade – especially if it's clear that the child made it. I had a cushion made for me once. It was badly sewn together (the stuffing was falling out) but it melted my heart.

A bottle of wine always goes down well.

Your social life at school

When your child starts school, it's not only them making new friends, but you too. Some parents take to this easily, whereas others, particularly those who are introverts, can feel like they've gone back to their own first few days at school, as they stand anxiously in the playground, waiting for somebody to talk to them.

I've always found it hard to speak to new people, and I was often the mum standing at the edge of the playground, trying to look busy, so I could hide my embarrassment at being alone, while praying that somebody would take me under their wing. The more my children grew, however, the more I realised that I was the one who had to make it happen. This is, of course, daunting if your instinct is to hide away, but I found that my children being at school gave me a great starting point, because I always had something in common with the other parents. I've also learned, over the years, that many others felt the same as me, waiting for somebody to speak to them and strike up a friendship.

If you find it hard to initiate conversations in person, then joining or setting up a parents' group online is a great idea. You can get to know other parents without the embarrassment of knowing what to say in person. If your school doesn't have a parents' chat group, then do give some thought to setting one up and suggesting a 'getting-to-know-you' event of some sort, like a coffee morning or evening meet-up. If you work and you're not around much for the school runs, then these get-togethers can be particularly invaluable.

As the school year progresses, it is inevitable that a playground clique or two will develop. Again, this can feel like being transported back to your own school days. I like to think the best of people, so I imagine that most people are too concerned about how others perceive them to worry about judging others, but there definitely are always a couple of parents who like to gossip. You won't ever change them, so the best course of action is to be pleasant to them, say 'Hi' and smile as you walk past, then leave them to it. You don't need these sorts of people in your life. Look for your tribe. Befriend those who make you feel good about yourself and share your outlook on life. The plus side here is that if your children become friends too, it's much more likely they will be better suited too.

Playdate etiquette

So your child has asked if their friend can come around to play after school – what should you do? Here are some points to note when arranging a playdate, or when your child has been invited to a friend's house:

- Speak to the other child's parents/carers first. If you cannot do this on the school run, give your child a piece of paper with your name and telephone number and a short note on it and get them to give it to the other child (better still, put it in the child's bag yourself), asking their parent to call or text you.

- If you can't get in contact with the other parent this way, then ask the school office, or your child's class teacher if they can pass your contact details on (they will not be able to give out the other parent's details for data-protection reasons).

- Once you have got in contact with the other child's parents, arrange a date and timings. Agree on whether you will drop the child home or the other parent will collect (unless you want to invite the parent to come too – this is absolutely not expected though, it's far more common for the child to come alone).

- If you do the school run by car, either make sure that you have a car seat for the other child (perhaps collecting it from their parent in the morning) or ask the parent if they can come to school to collect their child and drop them off at your house.

- Make sure you have emergency contact details for the child's parents and ask if there are any medical conditions or allergies you need to be aware of.

- There is no obligation to feed the other child, unless you have specifically invited them for dinner (in which case, make sure you ask the parent what they like to eat). It's always a good idea to have a snack on hand when you get home from school though, so again, make sure you know of any allergies/intolerances in advance.

- Most playdates last for no more than an hour or two, meaning that if they happen after school, they are usually finished by 5.30 p.m. at the latest. It's always best to start off short and build up to longer ones, especially those involving staying for dinner. I would not expect to have to give a child (and their parent if they were coming too) dinner unless they were staying until after 6 p.m.

- Don't feel that you have to arrange activities. The best playdates happen when children use their imaginations and entertain themselves. You may want to keep an ear out for awkward silences or bickering though, and suggest an activity if necessary, such as going in the garden, playing a board game, making something out of Lego or building blanket forts. Don't resist resorting to

TV if you need to; two hyped and tired children often need the little bit of downtime that this provides. No parent is going to judge you for enlisting the help of children's TV for half an hour.

- If the other child is upset or can't settle without their parent, don't be afraid to call and ask them to come back (and if it is your child at someone else's house, ask that they do the same). Just like settling in at school, some children take time to settle into playdates. Don't take it personally if the other child's parents have to collect them after only half an hour. My children have had so many abandoned playdates over the years.

- Children can often find it hard to share on playdates. If you suspect your child may not be happy to share their toys, then prepare with them in advance, asking them to sort out toys they don't want to share. You can then hide these away, so that there is no conflict when the other child tries to play with them at the playdate.

- Sleepovers don't tend to come into the equation until children have been at school for two or three years, but if you feel your child and their friend are ready for one there is no reason to delay. Similarly, if your child is invited to one and you know they won't cope, don't be afraid to politely decline.

- There does seem to be an unwritten rule that playdates should be reciprocated, but if your child does not want a child to return to their house or go to theirs, then it really is OK to turn down an invitation or just not offer to reciprocate. It's much better to avoid a potentially stressful situation than to feel the need to go through with it for fear of being viewed slightly negatively. The other parent may feel just as relieved as you.

Birthday and party etiquette

Your child may have been invited to a handful of birthday parties before starting school, but the invitations will probably now increase dramatically. It can often seem as though they have a party every other week during their first year at school. These new invitations can raise questions about birthday-party etiquette, including what to do when your child is celebrating their own birthday, particularly if it falls on a school day.

Treats at school

If a child's birthday falls on a school day, it is quite common for them to take in a treat of some form to share with the other children, cakes and sweets being the most common. Some parents avoid giving their children sugary or processed foods, but barring them when all the other children in the class are having them is a recipe for disordered eating later in life. The more we restrict more palatable food when children are younger, the less likely they are to be able to self-regulate when they are older. For this reason, I never prohibited my children from taking the birthday sweets or cakes that were given out at the end of the school day. If you are adamant that you don't want your child to eat these things though, then I would advise allowing your child to take what's on offer and then swap it out for something you think is appropriate once you're home from school; this makes the giver feel better and also doesn't single out your child. If they cannot eat certain foods for medical reasons, you may choose to leave one or two treats with the teacher, so that they can give out a safe item on days when other children are being given treats, thus ensuring that your child won't feel left out.

If you would like to give a little gift to all the children in your class when it's your own child's birthday, but want to avoid regular sweets and cakes, then you could give out fruit kebabs, some homemade ice lollies (in the summer), or some homemade energy balls or similar. (It is worth checking with your child's teacher in advance as to whether there are any special policies surrounding this if you intend giving the treats out on the school's premises.) If you would prefer your child to not give out anything then don't be swayed by any perceived pressure to do so.

Whom to invite?

When it comes to birthday celebrations, party planning can be fraught with tension when children start school because you are faced with inviting all the children in the class or picking only a select few. Either of these is OK: you shouldn't feel you have to invite all the children if space and funds don't stretch, or if you simply don't want to have to entertain thirty children (although some schools do recommend that if you are giving the invitations out at school, the whole class should be invited). I would, however, be careful that the children you don't invite don't feel excluded or that you don't accidentally offend their parents. The best way to do this is to invite less than half of the children in the class – that way, it's unlikely that any offence will be taken. For this reason, my own children's birthday celebrations have either included four to eight other children, or the whole class.

It's important to add here that there are nearly always one or two children who never seem to get invited to any celebrations – perhaps because they have a SEND that affects their behaviour and they are viewed as 'the naughty child', or they come from a difficult home life, which impacts on their interactions with others. Spare a thought for these children. It can be incredibly lonely for them, and their exclusion can actually make their behaviour at school worse. It is also terribly hard to be the parent of a so-called 'naughty' child who is never invited anywhere. Knowing that other children don't like your child is hard enough; knowing that other parents don't like them either is almost impossible to handle. Parties can be a great way to be completely inclusive and invite the child who is always left out. Don't underestimate the difference you could make to their life (and their parents') by inviting them.

When to invite

In terms of invitations, the standard practice is to send them out two to four weeks before the event, to give the other parents enough notice (but not so much that they forget about it). Make sure your address (or that of the venue, if the party is not at home), phone number and email address are all included and ask people to RSVP by a certain date if you need to finalise plans. Expect that at least a third will not RSVP though, and that some of those who say they're coming won't turn up on the day because of an unexpected change of plans or illness and so on.

Party bags

The tradition of giving out party bags is still strong, despite most of the contents ending up in the bin as soon as children get home. If you are conscious of your eco footprint and would like to reduce the amount of plastic that ends up in landfill, as well as avoiding the bag full of sugar that children get sent home with, but you would still like to send children home with a small memento, the following can work well:

- Buy a cheap multipack set of story books to give out.

- Set up an activity at the party whereby children can take home what they've made. For example, they can decorate plant pots and you can give out sunflower or cress seeds for them to grow at home.

- Make or buy cupcakes and ice them as a party activity, giving them out to children to take home at the end of the party.

- Make or decorate shop-bought party hats, masks or crowns.

- If there are any popular trading cards or stickers, give each child one pack to take home.

- A little pad of paper and a new pen or pencil always go down well.

- Give out screw-top jars with some dry cookie mix ingredients for children to bake at home.

- Buy some cheap paint-your-own children's ornaments or baubles for them to paint at the party and take home with them.

There is no need to feel that you have to send children home with anything, though. I think a lot of parents would be happy to lose the party-bag tradition and may well be relieved that someone else has been brave enough to take the plunge.

Birthday gifts

If your child is invited to a party, it is considered good etiquette to send them with a gift. However, many parents worry about how much they should spend. I think it is less about what you spend and more about the thought that you put in. Some of my children's favourite gifts over the years have been handmade. For instance, a hand-sewn glasses case, a jar of handmade fudge and a decorated photo frame with a picture of the two friends in it.

If handmade is not your thing and you would rather give something shop-bought, you could keep a supply of presents at the ready. When my children were little and were invited to a party seemingly every week, I used to stock up on little gifts in the January and summer sales or whenever I could find a bargain, along with multipacks of generic children's birthday cards and wrapping paper. That way, I always had a present in stock when a last-minute invite came in or I was running low on funds. The extra bonus here was that if my children were ever asked to donate to a school raffle, there was always something little they could take in.

This chapter has helped to explain and reassure you about the more social side of school – something that can often be left out of whatever you might read about preparing for school, but which I found to be key in helping me to feel calm and in control and, in turn, helping my children feel positive and to settle in. The next chapter will look at how to *stay* positive and help your child as they progress through school, including moving up to the next year and beyond.

Chapter 8

Looking to the Years Ahead

I t's never too soon to start thinking about the future of your child's schooling and how to keep things calm, balanced and happy over the next decade. In the initial rush to choose a school, prepare children and settle them in during the first few weeks, it can be hard to adopt a more long-term view. Holidays, homework, end-of-year tests, moving up a year and progressing to the next school stage can seem like a lifetime away. And thinking about secondary school seems ridiculous, when it feels like only yesterday that your child was a newborn bundle in your arms. But giving some thought now to the transitions ahead will ensure that the path to the future is as smooth as it can be – a future that will be here before you know it.

This chapter will cover those issues that don't crop up initially, in the first few weeks or months at school, and are therefore often forgotten altogether in school-preparation guides and articles. Having put so much effort and research into your choice of school and getting your child off to the best start possible, it makes no sense not to continue with the same approach to the rest of their schooling.

Striking a good school–home life balance

The first few months of school can result in lots of exhaustion, so it is best to avoid any clubs or extracurricular activities. Once your child has settled in though, and their body has adapted to a new daily rhythm, it may be appropriate to add in a few after-school activities. But be careful that you don't rush this transition. Some children really do need to just go home and relax after school, and this may be the case for several years. The best way to test whether your child can cope with after-school activities is to give them a try, but preferably without committing financially to a whole term's worth. The summer term, at the end of the first year, can be a good time to try adding new activities, as it's lighter for longer in the evenings and children have adapted well to school timings by then.

School-aged children need downtime at home, no matter how long they have been at school and how old they are. This includes time at the weekend and over school holidays. Many parents worry that their children aren't entertained enough, especially during the holidays, but this free time is so important. Unstructured time helps children to relax, recharge and restore. Try to resist scheduling every free day during half-term, winter, spring and summer holidays and use the time off for your child to get bored, rest and use their imaginations.

There is only one school-related activity that it is important to continue outside of school, and that is reading. Reading to and with your child is perhaps the most valuable use of free time. Research has shown that the frequency with which parents read with children has a significant effect on the outcomes of their schooling.[1] Regular daily reading to and with children between four and five years of age significantly improves not only their reading skills, but cognitive skills too, such as language and communication. In fact, this effect is so profound that the cognitive age of those who are read to every day is around a year older than that of children who are not read to regularly.

Reading school books vs reading for pleasure

While reading regularly with your children is undoubtedly important, many parents do not like the lacklustre and uninspiring books that are sent home from school. These books are usually accompanied by a reading record in which parents are supposed to write their observations of the child's reading. This reading practice is most definitely academic in focus, and therein lies the problem: while some children are happy to do their daily reading practice from school, others hate every minute of it. For the latter, persevering can be detrimental to their enjoyment of books. If you find yourself in a position where your child is resisting their reading practice, perhaps the best thing you can do is to return to sharing books that you enjoy together. The real predictor of reading ability is not powering through the Oxford Reading Tree levels, but how often you read to your child and how much they love books. A child who can ramp up the levels quickly, but who is bored and hates doing it will become one who shuns books for pleasure as they grow. A child who enjoys a bedtime book of their choosing with their parent every night, who actively enjoys being read to and exploring the text and pictures on the page, will be one who retains their love of reading for enjoyment as they grow.

What should you do if you decide to ditch the daily reading practice in favour of fostering an innate love of reading? Start with a chat with your child's teacher: explain your concerns and reassure them that you do read every day with your child, but that you won't be reading the schoolbooks or completing the reading record. I have never yet met a teacher who wasn't happy with this. Their concern is that children read regularly – what they read, and whether it is recorded in a book, is immaterial.

Are there any benefits to homework?

The first few months at school can often lull parents into a false sense of security, as homework is rarely set. If it is, it may be to draw a picture of the family or bring in some boxes for junk modelling. But after the first term, the dreaded work-sheets can often start to creep in. Although these and any topic-based assignments are a far cry from what your child will be set in junior or secondary school, they can still cause distress at home. If your child is happy to do the homework set by the school, then there is no problem. When children aren't happy, however – especially if they get upset and angry, resisting doing their homework – it is so important to speak to the school. Before doing this though, there are a few things you should know.

Is homework effective? The answer is yes – but there is a caveat. Homework is effective for children at secondary-school level (eleven years and older), but for those in infant and primary school the evidence is far less compelling.[2] There is very little benefit to regular homework for young children, and although those at schools where it is set do tend to perform better academically, this may have more to do with the general ethos, the teaching or even the demographics of the school than the homework itself.

While there is no benefit to homework for children at infant and primary school, it may well bring risks. If children can't cope with homework, their intrinsic motivation to work hard at school can be damaged and their enjoyment of learning be impaired. If homework becomes a weekly battle at home, this can bring anxiety and tension into a space that should be a safe haven, away from any stress at school. And it's not only children who can be impacted. Attempting to make a reluctant child sit down and do their homework can quickly become very draining for parents. The whole affair can eat into precious family time and leave parents resenting school. So if your child is a homework refuser or struggler, then it is important to speak to the class teacher. Most are aware that there is no proven benefit of homework at infant and junior level and, off the record, most will admit that they dislike setting it for young children.

With my children, I met up with their teachers and explained that my aim was to support both the school and my child, but if homework caused anxiety or stress at home, then we would not be completing it. I reassured the teacher that my child had plenty of learning opportunities outside of school, explaining that we would regularly read together, cook together, explore nature, do crafts and so on, and I never encountered any objection to this approach. As it happens, my children would often complete their homework of their own accord, especially if it was project- rather than worksheet-based. But they knew that I wouldn't force the issue if they really couldn't, or didn't want to, do it. As stated earlier, homework does have benefits at secondary level and, as my children grew older, we discussed this, explaining that they would need to do it at their next school. They all accepted this, and not enforcing homework at infant and junior school had no negative impact on their attitude to it when the time came.

Term-time holidays

Travel during term time is significantly cheaper than it is in the school holidays – often up to half or a third of the price. With this in mind, can you take your child out of school for holidays during the school term? The answer is yes – however, you may well have to pay a fine for unauthorised absence, as only time off for an 'exceptional circumstance' will be authorised. In England, at the time of writing, the fine for unauthorised absence is £60 per parent, per child. This is doubled if it is not paid within twenty-one days of being issued, and is likely to rise over the coming years, while the number of fines imposed is also rising sharply. Scotland and Northern Ireland do not impose a fine, at the time of writing, but are unlikely to grant a request for absence, while Welsh schools are able to grant up to ten days' (or two school weeks') holiday per school year.

But does taking children out school for a short family holiday really impact their education? While poor attendance absolutely has a negative effect on attainment, this cannot be compared with a family holiday, particularly one with an educational bias. A well-chosen holiday can not only provide some much-needed family downtime, it is also an opportunity to immerse a child in another culture, introducing them to new foods, new languages, history, nature, art and music. Arguably, a child could learn much more on a family holiday than they would learn during the same time at school.

Research published by the *Times Educational Supplement* found that there was no negative impact on performance at school when children were taken out for a two-week holiday.[3] In fact, they were actually more likely to reach the expected levels for their age at the end of the school year. This may, of course, be down to social or financial demographics, or the relationship with and attitudes of parents, but it does provide reassurance that term-time holidays for children who otherwise have good attendance are not as damaging as our governments would have us believe.

Are there any downsides to taking a term-time holiday (aside from a potential fine) if a child otherwise has good attendance? Yes, there can be. Time away from school can negatively impact friendships, particularly already fragile ones. Children can miss key messages and lessons and find it hard to catch up. (I missed lessons on multiplication as a young child when on holiday in Greece for a week and to this day I still struggle with it – something that may or may not be related to our family trip.) Term-time holidays can also cause stress and difficulty for teachers when they have to try to bring children up to speed on their return to school.

I don't think there is any one right or wrong answer here. You should weigh up what your child will miss out on versus what they could gain from the holiday and, of course, any financial implications too: it is likely that you would save far more on a term-time holiday – even taking the fine into account. I did take my children out of school very occasionally when they were much younger. They had otherwise good records and I tried to tag holidays on to the end or beginning of term, so they were less disruptive. I have not, and would not, however, take a child out of school for a holiday from the age of eleven onwards.

Standardised tests and other assessments

In standardised tests all children answer the same questions (or selection of questions) and the results are scored in a standardised way, so that they can be compared to those of other children at different schools and in other areas and, ultimately, assess children nationally. Standardised testing is commonly employed in many countries. In England, children sit SATs (standard attainment tests) in Year 6 (the last year of primary school) and currently Year 2, and then go on to take their GCSEs in year 11 (the last compulsory year of secondary school). Thankfully, after a lot of pressure and campaigning from both parents and those working in education, the UK government have recently announced that the Key Stage One SATs – used as a measure of proficiency of mathematics and English and taken when a child is seven years old – will no longer be statutory by 2023. However, there are new moves for more formal testing of school readiness and multiplication ability testing to be introduced. In comparison, in Finland – widely considered to be one of the best education systems in the world – there are no compulsory standardised tests until the end of high school. Standardised testing can be unbelievably stressful for children, particularly very young ones, and their use and efficacy have been heavily criticised.

How can you help children with SATs in the earlier years of school? The best course of action is to work on raising your child's self-esteem, so that they do not feel that they are reduced to a number on a piece of paper. Help your child to understand that you value everything about them, and that tests cannot possibly measure how kind they are, how funny they are, what a good friend they are and how much they enjoy art, music, dance or sport. Help them to implement the growth-mindset theory from an early age, taking the ideas on board and demonstrating them yourself. As they get older, explain that most of these standardised tests are a measure of the school, not of them individually, and that the results mean nothing to them or their future (because no matter what schools may say in the run-up to the SATs, the results are pretty meaningless to the children themselves). Above all else, take the pressure off: don't force revision or catch-up clubs; instead, focus on making sure your child's life is full of play, nature, travel, fun and wonder and that your home is a sanctuary from any academic pressure they may face at school.

Moving up to the next school year

It's amazing how quickly the first year of school flies by. Before you know it, January has arrived and quickly turns into the February half-term. By this point, your child is exactly halfway through their first year of school, but it feels as if you've all barely had a chance to stop and catch your breath. Once the spring term is in full force, thoughts start to turn to the next academic year and preparing children for their new classrooms and usually new teachers.

The second year of school can be a tricky transition, as the work starts to take on a more academic focus, with far less opportunity for free movement and play. Some children take this in their stride, while others react badly, even if their first year at school was calm and successful. In my experience, the only answer to these tricky transitions is time and patience. Moving into the second year of school is a big adjustment for little people. You may see a return of restraint collapse (see page 137) and their behaviour may regress at school too. Tiredness often increases as well. As with settling them into school initially, try to scale back their after-school activities for the first half of term and get plenty of relaxed downtime. Keep an eye on their sleep and don't put too much pressure on them at home. The more you ensure that your home, your arms and your words are an oasis of peace and calm, the quicker your child will adapt to the change. Teachers are very used to the difficulties some children can face with the transition to the next school year too, so do ask to meet with them and ask for any advice they can give too.

Most schools will put 'moving-up' sessions into place at the end of the school year, to prepare children for their new teachers and classrooms when they return in the new school year. These sessions are very important in helping your child to settle, so if you are going to book a term-time holiday, make sure that you schedule it to avoid them. Without the familiarity this important preparation can provide, children may not settle easily with their new teacher.

What if you move away and your child needs to change schools?

Despite the best-laid plans, life happens. Perhaps you already know that your child will be changing school soon after they start – if, for instance, you're a military family. Sometimes the move comes unexpectedly. So what should you do if you find yourself needing to change your child's school?

The best place to start is to return to the beginning of this book. Preparation for moving schools is no different from preparation for starting in the first place. Focus on familiarising your child with the buildings and the staff, and visit as often as you can in advance. If this is not possible, share lots of photos (of both the buildings and staff) with your child and make sure they are used to their new uniform well before they start.

Arrange to meet up with some of their new classmates and their parents for playdates if this is feasible. Seeing a familiar face or two on the first day really helps to reduce the anxiety that can so often accompany being 'the new kid'. As well as getting to know new children, it can help to keep in touch with their old classmates – with playdates, if the move is not too far away or writing letters and video chatting, if it is. Holding on to a relationship with their old friends, while forming new ones is so important to ease children into the transition.

It's not only your child who needs to adapt though; it's important for you to make some new friends and build a relationship with the new school too. Joining the PTA is perfect for this, and although it can be daunting to walk into a room of people who already know each other, it's definitely the quickest way to get to know other parents. As ever, patience, understanding and compassion are needed while your child adjusts (and you too).

If the move to a new school also includes moving to a new house, it is understandable for children to be sad and anxious for several weeks, even months, after, but their sadness and anxiety may express itself in ways you wouldn't expect. Angry and violent behaviour and rudeness towards you can be common. This will pass in time; try not to take it personally until it does. If your child is still struggling with the transition after several months, it can be worth speaking to your family doctor or the school SENCo to see if there is any extra support that may be available, such as counselling or a support group.

SECONDARY SCHOOL – AND WHEN TO START THINKING ABOUT IT

This might seem like an odd inclusion in a book about starting school for the very first time. Why would you even begin to think about secondary school now? I used to think the same and was frequently flummoxed when my friends, with three- and four-year-olds (not even at infant school yet) started talking about the high schools they hoped their children would eventually attend. I asked them why they would possibly consider it so soon, to which they replied, 'Well, where you live decides on the school your child will go to, and where you are now is in catchment for a pretty poor secondary. Are you thinking of staying here?' I was happy with the local infant and primary schools and it seemed ridiculous to think any further ahead than that, but shortly after this, we found ourselves looking to move to a new house (for other reasons) and I wondered if I should think about what they were saying. I researched online and found that families did indeed often move with the sole aim of living in catchment for the best secondaries in the area. And while we did take this into account when buying our new home, it wasn't a major factor. I wanted a house we would be happy in for a long time and one that could grow with us as a family. Having said that, I am so pleased we did factor in secondary-school catchments because, as it turned out, we ended up living in the right location to pretty much guarantee our top choice of secondary school. And I noticed that many parents near by would frantically try to move when their children were in Year Five or Six, after realising that they had no hope of getting their children into their preferred school.

Aside from living in the 'right' catchment area, another important impact of where we lived was that the infant and junior school was a feeder for the local secondary. This meant that the schools had strong links and the younger children would visit the secondary often, for music, art, drama, dance and sporting events. By the time they were approaching their final year at junior school, they all knew the secondary school well and felt at home there already. This was very helpful when it came to the ultimate transition to 'big school' and settling in.

So when should you consider your child's secondary schooling? I genuinely believe it's never too soon. Of course, schools can and do change. Heads can join and leave, official scores go up and down and there is no guarantee that a school you love now will be the same in six or seven years' time. Similarly, a school you are not keen on now may have a complete turnaround by the time your child is old enough to attend. Nevertheless, it is worth giving the choice of secondary at least a cursory glance right at the start of your child's education.

Raising an inspired learner

When I was researching what to include in this chapter, I asked parents what advice they would have liked to receive to help them and their children flourish throughout the school years, long after the initial transition to starting school. The most popular suggestion was 'how to keep them loving learning as they get older'. This is almost impossible to address, but I think the key lies in how you yourself view education and how you inspire and support your child. The following are all important influences:

- **Focus on the positives of school** Even if you have concerns, discuss the best bits the most with your child.

- **Talk to your child about your own learning journey** What did you enjoy at school? What are they doing that you wish you could have done?

- **Read with them and to them (books that they want to read)** A love of reading is perhaps the best gift you can bestow on your child. The best way to raise a child who loves to read as they grow is for them to see you reading regularly for pleasure. Remember, you are their biggest role model.

- **Encourage natural curiosity** The constant 'Why?' questions can be so draining when children are little, but as hard as it may be to answer, and as tempted as you may be to tell them to stop asking questions, encourage them as much as you can. The minute a child stops asking questions is the moment their love of learning starts to wane.

- **Explore with them** Get outdoors – explore the natural world, your local surroundings and further afield.

- **Nurture their interests** If your child is a budding palaeontologist, for instance, feed their fascination with visits to museums, conversation and other resources.

- **Encourage a growth mindset (see page 12)** Help children to be resilient and not to give up in the face of failure. Discuss your own failures with them and how you ultimately overcame them.

- **Work on their self-esteem** A child who feels good about themselves is one who will be more open to learning. Praise their efforts more than their achievements – especially the times when they don't succeed, but put lots of work in.

- **Hold back on the pressure** While you may love your child to be top of the class, they may not share your goal, even if they are naturally gifted. It's OK for them to be average.

- **Value the arts and sports as much as academic study** Children who have well-rounded interests are usually happier. The arts and sports can give a child a chance to shine who may not otherwise do so in academic study.

- **Make home a restful sanctuary (see page 132)** Dial back on any nagging to complete homework, revise for tests or prepare for projects and presentations, and understand that children should feel safe to be their authentic selves with you. This may mean unpleasant behaviour but offloading with you allows them to 'hold things in' at school.

- **Resolve any bullying as quickly as possible (see page 136)** Don't put up with bullying behaviour towards your child – from other children or from teachers.

- **Be mindful of undiagnosed SENDs (see page 144)** Trust your instinct (in spite of what school may say) if you have an inkling that your child may have a SEND. Push for a second opinion or referral for your child to get the recognition and support that they deserve.

- **Get involved with the school community (see page 166)** The happiest children at school have parents who have built a good relationship with the school and who get involved with all elements of their education and work, with the school to support them.

I'm sure there are many more points that could be added to this list, but delving into your own memory bank and asking yourself, 'What did I need (or not need) when I was their age?' will perhaps provide the best answer to the question of how to raise an inspired learner – you already know the answer because you've already been there!

The best parenting is always a balance of both the short- and the long-term view, and starting school is no different. This chapter has, hopefully, helped you to take a brief glimpse into the years ahead, while also giving you some insight for today.

Chapter 9

What Teachers (and Parents) Wish Parents Knew Before Starting School

When writing this book, I spoke to hundreds of teachers and parents of older children and asked them what advice they had for parents of new school starters. I also asked parents what they wish they had been told before their own children started school. Initially, I had planned to weave their observations throughout the book, but they were so useful, I thought that they warranted a section of their own. So for this chapter, I'm going to hand over to the teachers and a group of parents who were once in your shoes. I am extremely grateful for their comments and hope that their words will reassure you.

From the mouths of teachers . . .

I asked teachers what they wish they could tell parents about school readiness and what it means. Here are their thoughts:

. . . on school readiness

I think parents understanding what 'school readiness' really means is so important. It doesn't mean teaching children how to read or write before they are ready. It's about making sure they can dress themselves (it's not uncommon to end up with a ten-minute PE lesson, because the rest of the session is taken up with helping children dress and undress) and being interested in the world around them.

Reading to your child, singing, nursery rhymes and talking to your child are the best things you can do for your child academically at home.

I would love all parents to know that personal, social and emotional development outweigh any other area of learning at school starting age – these skills are the building blocks for success in all other areas of learning.

Please don't try to teach children to read or write before they start school. Often parents teach kids the letter names or say the sounds wrongly (the way they might have learned themselves as a child) and we have to undo it all.

I always tell parents to focus on teaching their children independence skills, such as dressing and undressing, how to use the toilet alone, turn taps on and off, how to put on and take off their shoes and recognise their name. Of course, it doesn't matter if they can't do all of that when they begin school, but it's a good place to start preparing them if they are ready.

Don't worry about teaching numbers; just count ordinary things during the day and definitely *don't* buy any hideous workbooks to do with them.

I wish parents knew that fine motor skills are vital for writing success. Playing at home with Play-Doh, Lego, board games, tearing paper, cooking (stirring and kneading), cutting with scissors, playing with nuts and bolts, tongs and tweezers and chopsticks, threading, using spray bottles and playing finger games (such as 'Incy Wincy Spider') are all important ways to develop the strength and dexterity children will need when they start school. They can't write or hold a pencil properly if they don't have enough hand strength.

... on practical preparations and purchases

I asked teachers what they wish they could tell parents to buy (and not to buy) and prepare before their children start school. This is what they told me:

It would really help if the children could come to school with *everything* named.

Please don't send your child to school in lace-up shoes, unless they can tie them independently.

Don't buy lots of expensive brands to dress your children in. They will – and should – get messy at school! This means they are learning and exploring.

I wish parents understood that uniform does, sadly, get lost. We know parents get very upset by this. Unfortunately, with thirty children in a class, teachers can't keep track of it all. Please label, label, label to help us out.

When you go shopping in the summer holidays for PE bags, school bags, coats, lunch bags make sure your child sees them before their first day. I always have a couple of chil-_dren in September who get really upset because they don't know which is their lunch box because they have never seen it before.

. . . on children's emotions, settling in and making friends

Several teachers expressed their views about the settling-in process and friendships, and the reassurance they wanted to pass on to new school-starter parents:

I wish parents knew that it's OK for children to be shy; they're all so different and young still. It's OK for them to feel nervous in a new environment. But also, once Mum and Dad leave the room, they often have so much fun they forget their nerves!

I would emphasise that starting school is a *huge* milestone. Your child will be exhausted after school each day and will need plenty of downtime and TLC. Extra clubs after school will be too much for most children in their first year at school.

I want parents to know that every child is an individual. Don't compare your child to any other in their year group or class. It puts unnecessary pressure on you as a parent and on the child. And don't try to second-guess their academic 'ranking' either. Children love learning – just let them enjoy the process without the pressure.

I wish parents knew not to lose heart if their child hasn't found a friend – or a group of friends – straight away. It doesn't mean that they're not liked; it's more that they are learning to develop social and cooperative play skills.

I would like to reassure parents of the young children that I have taught that if their child is upset leaving them at the school gates, 99 per cent of the time they are absolutely fine within a couple of minutes. They are so busy that they just get on with it. I've spoken to so many parents that have been worried that their child has cried all day – but they haven't.

I wish that parents knew how important it was to celebrate their child's independence. It is such a huge milestone for parents when their child starts school and I completely understand their fear of them growing up too quickly. Combat your feelings by smothering them with cuddles and kisses at home, rather than waiting until you're in the playground. When they are inside the school grounds, encourage them to walk in and to carry their own posses-sions and hang their own things on their peg; please don't be tempted to follow them in and do it for them. If they can be a little bit independent at the start of the school day, they will get on so much better at school and find it much easier and more enjoyable. I know it's hard, but letting them own their independence really does set them up well for life.

... on expectations and communication with parents moving forward

Here's what teachers told me about their relationships with parents and what they wish they knew or could change:

Don't worry about reading their school books repeatedly. Read them once or twice and then read more widely.

We would love you to share your talents with the school. You never know when your skills might come in handy for a project e.g. cake-making, sewing, music, etc.

I would love parents to know that communication and openness are vital to securing a good relationship with your child's school. Talk things through instead of worrying about them and don't let things trouble you. A problem shared is a problem halved! Children will feel supported and loved by everyone if we work as a team and have the same goals and expectations for them.

Please don't send your child into school if they are unwell.

Please don't be on your mobile phone when you drop off and pick up your child from school.

Please talk to us! Please keep teachers in the loop about what's been happening at home (both positive and negative), so that we can support you and your child.

. . . on their own feelings

Finally, I asked the teachers what they wish parents knew about how they felt, as teachers:

> I wish parents knew that on the first day of the school year, we are often really nervous too. Most teachers I know wake up multiple times the night before meeting all the new kids and parents from nerves/excitement. It's like starting a brand-new job every year (but we wouldn't change it for the world).

> Teachers wish that parents knew that we genuinely care for your children and we want to work in partnership with you to improve outcomes for them.

> I wish parents knew that teachers are humans too and that we do have a life outside the classroom.

> I wish all parents to know that teachers care about children and want them to fulfil their potential. We spend evenings, weekends and the middle of the nights trying to plan exciting lessons and think of new ways to support your little ones.

> I wish that all parents realised that we are on the same side – that we all want what's best for each child, that we work better and the children are happier if we are all reading from the same page.

From the mouths of parents . . .

I also spent time talking with many parents, both of new school starters and some whose children are much further along their education journey. I asked them what they wish they had known when their children started school and what they would pass on to parents who are standing where they once were:

. . . on school readiness

Here is what parents thought about practical preparations and the idea of school readiness:

My son had just turned four three weeks before he started school. I wish I had taken the decision for him to go part-time as he is shattered every day now and has had a few meltdowns after school due to this. It's so sad to see. He loves school, though, which is a good thing and has learned so much. But if I could go back, then I would definitely have let him go part-time.

My daughter is summer-born and I'd been so worried about her starting school so young, as she seemed to be behind everyone else, but she has done amazingly well and has never struggled. I know it's different for all kids, but I'd say give it a try.

I wish I'd known that it doesn't matter if they seem behind with not being able to write their names yet, or even sing their ABCs. This can all change within a few weeks.

... on practical preparations and purchases

Here's what parents had to say about the practical preparation side of things:

> I wish I'd known that more expensive uniform isn't necessarily better. Our supermarket purchases have lasted a lot longer than the more expensive ones and they wash better too.

> I wish my daughter had worn her shoes for a while before starting school. Instead we kept them as new and they really hurt her feet once she started.

> I wish I had bought stick-on name labels that actually stuck!

> I wish that I had waited to get his uniform when all the shops were running special offers. I thought I was being clever buying early, but I ended up paying more.

... on their children's emotions, settling in and making friends

Next, I asked parents how they helped their children to settle in to school and what they would do differently in retrospect. Here are their answers:

> I wish I had been made aware of the emotional outbursts that come from the 'let down' after school. We are two terms in and still have after-school meltdowns most nights.

I wish I had known how tired they would be, not just physically but emotionally and mentally. And I wish I had known how to handle that at the time.

Be positive and happy – make it an exciting place for them to go. Talk about your own time at school in a positive way, even if it wasn't such a positive experience for you.

I wish I'd known how important reconnection is after the school day.

I wish I'd known that toilet training could regress through the distraction of being at school. My son was completely dry from three years old, but wet every day at school for the first month. It was a shock because he had always been so good at asking and going to the toilet at home.

I'm glad that I eventually followed my gut and stopped swimming lessons for a bit, so we weren't rushing around after school.

I wish I'd known that my son would be fine! I was so worried about my shy little boy and how he would manage, but he has blossomed. He is so much more confident now; his social skills have developed so much. School has been the best thing for him.

When you collect them at the end of the day, always, *always* take a snack.

I wish I'd known not to bombard them with a million questions on the way home – they do not want to talk about their day. My four-year-old is ready to tell me everything he has done in the day when he is in bed. I've had to learn to be patient at this point too, and not to rush him just because it's time to sleep. I now know to start bedtime fifteen minutes or so earlier, which gives him the time to talk.

I wish I'd known that not all children will be tired – mine had lots of energy to burn at the end of the school day.

I wish I'd been aware of 'end-of-termitis', when children get tired and run down, with worsening behaviour towards the end of term – and how it's ongoing and doesn't just apply to the first year of school!

... on expectations and communication with the school and other parents moving forward

I also asked parents what advice they had for after the initial settling-in period, as children progress through the school. This is what they told me:

I wish I'd known that you don't have to make them do the homework.

The more you get involved and support your child's school, the better place it will be. So offer to listen to readers, sharpen the pencils, take the staples out of the display boards at the end of term. If you're buying ice creams for your kids on a hot day, get one extra for the teacher. And if you're too busy and work full-time, then join the PTA and support the evening events instead. It's the community of kids, teachers and parents working together that makes a school special.

Make friends with the other parents because they're the ones who will remind you about the plays, the book sharing, the spelling lists, the Forest School, mufti days and so on.

I wish I had joined the PTA earlier; being on the committee helped me so much in making friends with the other parents.

... on their own feelings

Finally, I chatted with parents about their own feelings – how they handled the transition and what advice they would give to parents knowing what they know now:

I'd like parents to know that it really will be OK. I was in pieces about sending my daughter to school and was contemplating home-educating. In the end, after much deliberating, I decided that we should fully immerse our-selves into the whole school thing. She has *loved* it and has grown so much this past year. I was expecting to resent school and wish I hadn't sent her, but our first two terms have been full of joy.

You will cry on their first day – take tissues!

I wish I'd known that it might just be easier than I expected. And that filling my own head with horror stories of broken, exhausted children and bullying would not be helpful prepa-ration. We've had a few difficult mornings, but none of us are morning people, so that's to be expected. Apart from that it's gone really well.

I wish I had known how little I would know about their day. You go from nursery, where you get a full rundown of what they have done all day, what they have eaten and who they have played with to being told nothing when you pick them up. It's quite an adjustment.

I wish I'd known that I would actually love that my son has this little world away from me – he's always needed me a lot, so it is wonderful to see him have his little bits of independence.

I wish I had known just how emotional it all is. Not just for the children, but the parents too.

I hope that you have found the tips, advice and reflections in this chapter useful. As I was speaking to the parents and teachers, I found myself nodding frantically, agreeing with them wholeheartedly and repeatedly. The benefit of hindsight is a wonderful thing, but it is so much more useful when you can use your experiences to help others – which is why these observations will help you and your child, not just now, but for many years ahead.

A Closing Note

Do you remember your school's motto? Mine was *'Sic itur ad astra'* (you may have noticed it at the very front of this book). At the time I didn't care for Latin at all and had no idea what it meant, nor any desire to find out. It was only recently that I learned what it means: 'Thus one goes to the stars'. Learning this as an adult, I found it incredibly touching, and I was instantly reminded of a scene from Roald Dahl's *Matilda*, where the wonderful teacher Miss Honey speaks to Matilda about her love of reading books:

'You seemed so far away,' Miss Honey whispered, awestruck.

'Oh, I was. I was flying past the stars on silver wings,' Matilda said. 'It was wonderful.'

This, to me, sums up everything school should be to children: full of awe, wonder, inspiration, curiosity and the innately driven desire to do and be better. The goal is to foster a love of learning for life, preferably nurtured by teachers as amazing as Miss Honey (and avoiding any potential Trunchbulls). I think schools, and our education system in general, come under a lot of unnecessary criticism (albeit some that is sadly deserved). With the right school, the right teachers, the right support and the right approach to choosing, preparing for and settling in,

however, children can and will soar. I hope that this book has equipped you to help your child reach for the stars and to join them on some of that wonderful journey of discovery yourself. Good luck!
Sarah

References

Chapter 1

1. Ng, B., 'The neuroscience of growth mindset and intrinsic motivation', *Brain Science*, 8(2), 20 (February 2018).
2. Henderlong, J. and Lepper, M., 'The effects of praise on children's intrinsic motivation: A review and synthesis', *Psychological Bulletin*, vol. 128, no. 5 (2002), pp. 774–95.
3. Mondschein, E., Adolph, K. and Tamis-LeMonda, C., 'Gender bias in mothers' expectations about infant crawling', *Journal of Experimental Child Psychology*, 77 (2000), pp. 304–16; Aznar, A., 'Gender and age differences in parent–child emotion talk', *British Journal of Developmental Psychology*, vol. 33, issue 1 (2015), pp. 148–55.
4. OECD, PISA 2012 results: 'The ABC of gender equality in education: Aptitude, behaviour, confidence', (2013); Department for Education and Skills, 'Gender and education: The evidence on pupils in England' (2009).
5. Sullivan, A., Joshi, H. and Leonard, D., 'Single sex schooling and academic attainment at school and through the life course', *American Educational Research Journal*, 47 (2010), pp. 6–36.
6. Spielhofer, T., Benton, T. and Schagen, S., 'A study of the effects of school size and single-sex education in English schools', Research Papers in Education 19 (2004), pp. 133–59; Daly, P., 'The effects of single-sex and coeducational schooling on girls' achievement', Research Papers in Education 11 (1996), pp. 289–306.
7. Department for Education, 'Education and training statistics for the UK: 2017'.
8. Neugebauer, M., Helbig, M. and Landmann, A., 'Unmasking the myth of the same-sex teacher advantage', *European Sociological Review*, vol. 27, issue 5 (October 2011), pp. 669–89.
9. Spilt, J., Koomen, H. and Jak, S., 'Are boys better off with male

and girls with female teachers? A multilevel investigation of measurement invariance and gender match in teacher–student relationship quality', *Journal of School Psychology*, vol. 50, issue 3 (2012), pp. 363–78.

10. Blatchford, P., Goldstein, H., Martin, C. and Browne, W. 'A study of class size effects in English school reception year classes', *British Educational Research Journal*, 28(2) (2002), pp. 169–85; Hattie, J., 'The paradox of reducing class size and improving learning outcomes', *International Journal of Educational Research*, 43 (2005), pp. 387–425; Fredriksson, P., Öckert, B. and Oosterbeek, H., 'Long-term effects of class size', *Quarterly Journal of Economics*, 128(1) (2013), pp. 249–85.

11. Hargreaves, L., Comber, C. and Galton, M., 1996. 'The national curriculum: Can small schools deliver? Confidence and competence levels of teachers in small rural primary schools'. *British Educational Research Journal*, 22(1): 89-99; Hayes, D., 1999, 'Organising learning in mixed age classes: A case study about a multitask lesson', *Curriculum* 20(2) (1999), pp. 100–9.

12. Education Policy Institute, Social Mobility and Vulnerable Learners, 'How many children have SEND?', Policy Summary (24 November 2017).

13. Dee, T. and Sievertsen, H., 'The gift of time? School starting age and mental health', NBER Working Paper no. 21610 (October 2015).

14. Bedard, K. and Dhuey, E., 'The persistence of early childhood maturity: International evidence of long-run age effects', *Quarterly Journal of Economics*, 121(4) (2006), pp. 1437–72.

15. Black, S., Devereux, P. and Salvanes, K., 'Too young to leave the nest? The effects of school starting age', *Review of Economics and Statistics*, 93(2) (2011), pp. 455–67.

16. Muhlenweg, A., Blomeyer, A., Stichnoth, H. and Laucht, M., 'Effects of age at school entry (ASE) on the development of non-cognitive skills: Evidence from psychometric data,' *Economics of Education Review*, 31(3) (2012), pp. 68–76.

17. Kern, M. and Friedman, H., 'Early educational milestones as predictor of lifelong achievement, midlife adjustment and longevity', *Journal of Applied Developmental Psychology*, 30(4) (2008), pp. 419–30.

18. Schweinhart, L., Montie, J., Xiang, Z., Barnett, W., Belfield, C. and Nores, M., 'Lifetime effects: The High/Scope Perry Preschool Study through age 40', *High/Scope Press Educational Research Foundation* (2005), pp. 194–215.

19. Suggate, S., Schaughency, E. and Reese., E., 'Children learning to read later catch up to children reading earlier', *Early Childhood Research Quarterly*, 28 (2013), pp. 33–48.

20. Hannay, T., 'The effects of age, gender and school type on primary maths and reading attainment', SchoolDash report (2018).

21.   Cirin, R. and Lubwama, J., 'Delayed school admissions for summer born pupils', research report, Department for Education (May 2018).

Chapter 2

1.   Cirin, R. and Lubwama, J., 'Delayed school admissions for summer born pupils', research report, Department for Education (May 2018).
2.   Welsh Government, School Admission Code, Statutory Code document no: 005/2013 Accessed online: https://gov.wales/sites/default/files/publications/2018-03/school-admissions-code.pdf
3.   Marian, V. and Shook, A., 'The cognitive benefits of being bilingual', *Cerebrum*, 13 (September–October 2012).
4.   'Growing up in Scotland: Early experiences of primary school report' (https://www.gov.scot/publications/growing-up-scotland-early-experiences-primary-school/pages/4/).

Chapter 3

1.   Office for National Statistics, 'Births 2012 to 2017' (November 2016).

Chapter 5

1.   National Sleep Foundation Guidelines, 2015. Accessed online 24/6/19: https://www.sleepfoundation.org/press-release/national-sleep-foundation-recommends-new-sleep-times
2.   Lebourgeois, M., Wright, K., Lebourgeois, H. and Jenni, O., 'Dissonance between parent-selected bedtimes and young children's circadian physiology influences night-time settling difficulties', *Mind Brain Education* 7(4) (December 2013), pp. 234–42.
3.   Kohjama, J., Mindell, J. and Sadeh, A., 'Sleep characteristics of young children in Japan: Internet study and comparison with other Asian countries', *Pediatrics International*, 53(5) (October 2011), pp. 649–55.
4.   Mindell, J., Telofski, L., Wiegand, B. and Kurtz, E., 'A nightly bedtime routine: Impact on sleep in young children and maternal mood', *SLEEP*, vol. 32, no. 5 (2009).
5.   Peirano, P., Algarín, C., Chamorro, R. and Reyes, S. et al., 'Sleep and neurofunctions throughout child development: Lasting effects of early iron deficiency', *Journal of Pediatric Gastroenterology and Nutrition*, 48 suppl. 1 (March 2009), S8–15; Chollet, D., Franken, P., Raffin Y., Henrotte, J., Widmer, J. et al., 'Magnesium involvement in sleep: Genetic and nutritional models', *Behavior Genetics*, 31(5) (September 2001), pp. 413–25.

6. Montgomery, P., Burton, J., Sewell, R., et al., 'Fatty acids and sleep in UK children: Subjective and pilot objective sleep results from the DOLAB study: A randomized controlled trial', *Journal of Sleep Research*, 23(4) (August 2014), pp. 364–88.

7. Watson, E., Coates, A., Banks, S. and Kohler, M., 'Total dietary sugar consumption does not influence sleep or behaviour in Australian children', *International Journal of Food Sciences and Nutrition*, 69(4) (June 2018), pp. 503–12.

8. Martyn, D., McNulty, B., Nugent, A. and Gibney, M., 'Food additives and preschool children', *Proceedings of the Nutrition Society*, 72(1) (February 2013), pp. 109–16.

9. Hale, L. and Guan, S., 'Screen time and sleep among school-aged children and adolescents: A systematic literature review', *Sleep Medicine Reviews*, 21 (June 2015), pp. 50–8.

10. Butler, R. and Heron, J., 'The prevalence of infrequent bedwetting and nocturnal enuresis in childhood. A large British cohort', *Scandinavian Journal of Urology and Nephrology*, 42(3) (2008), pp. 257–64.

Chapter 8

1. Kalb, G. and van Ours, J., 'Reading to Young Children: A Head Start in Life', Melbourne Institute Working Paper no. 17/13 (2013).

2. Dettmers, S., Trautwein, U. and Ludtke, O., 'The relationship between homework time and achievement is not universal: evidence from multilevel analyses in 40 countries', *School Effectiveness and School Improvement*, 20(4) (2009), pp. 375–405; Gustafsson, J., 'Causal inference in educational effectiveness research: a comparison of three methods to investigate effects of homework on student achievement', *School Effectiveness and School Improvement*, 24:3 (2013), pp. 275–95; Cooper, H., Robinson, J.C. and Patall, E.A., 'Does homework improve academic achievement? A synthesis of research 1987–2003', *Review of Educational Research*, vol. 76, issue 1 (2006), pp. 1–62; Rønning, M., 'Who benefits from homework assignments?' *Economics of Education Review*, 30 (2011), pp. 55–64.

3. 'Term-time holidays "do not harm primary test scores"', *Times Educational Supplement* (26 October 2016).

Resources

Deferring school start date

Summer Born campaign: www.summerbornchildren.org

Upstart Scotland: www.upstart.scot

Country-specific information

England school applications:
www.gov.uk/apply-for-primary-school-place

NI school applications: www.eani.org.uk

Scottish Gaelic-medium Schools finder:
http://fdp.gaidhlig.scot/en/maps/

Home-education

Home Education UK: www.home-education.org.uk

Gov.UK on home-education: www.gov.uk/home-education

Education Otherwise: www.educationotherwise.org

Home-education groups in the UK: home-ed.info/local_groups

Alternative schooling

Montessori schools database:
www.montessori.org.uk/schools

Steiner schools finder:
www.steinerwaldorf.org/steiner-schools/list-of-schools

Democratic Education UK directory:
www.democraticeducation.co.uk

Private schooling

Independent Schools Association: www.isaschools.org.uk

Independent Schools Council: www.isc.co.uk

Gender-stereotyping

Delusions of Gender: The Real Science Behind Sex Differences,
Cordelia Fine, Icon Books (2011)

A Mighty Girl: books and movies for smart, confident,
courageous girls: www.amightygirl.com

Let Toys be Toys: campaign to persuade retailers to stop
categorising toys by gender: www.lettoysbetoys.org.uk

SEND

IPSEA: independent legal advice, support and training to help
get the right education for children with SEND:
www.ipsea.org.uk

Gov.UK SEND advice for parents:
www.gov.uk/government/publications/send-support-easy-
read-guide-for-parents

Sense: support, advice and information for families of children with complex disabilities: www.sense.org.uk

Contact: contact.org.uk

Bullying Resources

Bullying UK: www.bullying.co.uk/bullying-at-school

Supportline: www.supportline.org.uk/problems/bullying-at-school/

Gov.UK School Bullying advice: www.gov.uk/bullying-at-school

Childhood illnesses – advice and information

Threadworms: www.nhs.uk/conditions/threadworms

Head lice: www.nhs.uk/conditions/head-lice-and-nits

Hand-foot-and-mouth disease: www.nhs.uk/conditions/hand-foot-mouth-disease/

Chickenpox: www.nhs.uk/conditions/chickenpox/

Recommended further reading for parents

Mindset: Changing the Way You Think to Fulfil Your Potential, Carol S. Dweck, Robinson (2017)

Punished by Rewards, Alfie Kohn, Houghton Mifflin (1999)

Lost and Found: Helping Behaviorally Challenging Students (And While You're at It, All the Others), Ross Greene, Jossey Bass (2016)

How Children Learn: 50th Anniversary Edition, John Holt, Da Capo Lifelong Books (2017)

'Lives in the Balance' for parents and families:
https://www.livesinthebalance.org/parents-families

Recommended further reading for teachers

'Lives in the Balance' tour for educators:
www.livesinthebalance.org/walking-tour-educators

'Pivotal Education': https://pivotaleducation.com

When the Adults Change Everything Changes: Seismic Shifts in School Behaviour, Paul Dix, Independent Thinking Press (2017)

Restorative Justice Council:
http://restorativejustice4schools.co.uk

Recommended books for children

Starting School, Allan and Janet Ahlberg, Picture Puffins (2013)

Going to School, Anna Civardi, Usborne First Experiences (2005)

Stuff to Know when you Start School, DK Children (2018)

Starting School, Caryn Jenner, Franklin Watts (2012)

Sarah Ockwell-Smith

Website and blog: www.sarahockwell-smith.com

Instagram: www.instagram.com/sarahockwellsmith

Facebook: www.facebook.com/sarahockwellsmithauthor

Twitter: www.twitter.com/thebabyexpert

Index

Note: page numbers in **bold** refer to diagrams and page numbers in *italics* refer to information contained in tables.